D0081210

TWAYNE'S WORLD AUTHORS SERIES

A Survey of the World's Literature

FRANCE

Henry de Montherlant

(*TWAS 37*)

TWAYNE'S WORLD AUTHORS SERIES (TWAS)

The purpose of TWAS is to survey the major writers —novelists, dramatists, historians, poets, philosophers, and critics—of the nations of the world. Among the national literatures covered are those of Australia, Canada, China, Eastern Europe, France, Germany, Greece, India, Italy, Japan, Latin America, New Zealand, Poland, Russia, Scandinavia, Spain, and the African nations, as well as Hebrew, Yiddish, and Latin Classical literatures. This survey is complemented by Twayne's United States Authors Series and English Authors Series

The intent of each volume in these series is to present a critical-analytical study of the works of the writer; to include biographical and historical material that may be necessary for understanding, appreciation, and critical appraisal of the writer; and to present all material in clear, concise English—but not to vitiate the scholarly content of the work by doing so.

Henry de Montherlant

By ROBERT B. JOHNSON
University of Massachusetts

Twayne Publishers, Inc. :: New York

Library of Congress Catalog Card Number 67-25202

To Patricia

MANUFACTURED IN THE UNITED STATES OF AMERICA

Preface

The extensive works of Henry de Montherlant often seem at present to be cast in the shadows of the twentieth century. Because of his heroic-poetic language, they suggest a remoteness from current literary trends; their apparent ultra-conservatism recalls but never imitates what might be termed a "classical" focus of attention; and his vast *dramatis personae* wrought both from the past and the contemporary can impress us as denatured realities. On the contrary, however, Montherlant's insights frequently parallel those of our century. Like many of his contemporaries he is deeply concerned with man's condition, and he creates his own "universal man." He is a keen observer of man's psychological truths, whether in terms of his formation, his ecstasies and fancies, his obstacles, or his fate. Contrary to popular opinion, Montherlant creates not only heroic man seeking a very personal salvation, but also nonheroic man irrevocably bound to the chaos of life. Without being an existentialist he captures in his works the dilemma of man faced simply with life.

A study of Montherlant's works is a journey into another world containing at one pole the lyric ecstasy of youth and at the other pole the nihilistic despair of old age. At the poles and between them Montherlant's universal man moves in his strange solitary existence at the brink of a dream and at the edge of darkness. What is most maddening about such a universal man, however, is his truth, his verisimilitude. The long dialogue between Montherlant and his critics and public has been essentially one about the meaning of truth at once uncomfortable and uncompromising.

In forming what I believe to be a fresh view of Montherlant, I have abandoned extremes of criticism that either give to his works values they do not possess, or else mistakenly underestimate the real values they do contain. In addition to examining his major works, I have underlined in the first chapter the dilemma posed by Montherlant's unusual study of man, and I have closed this volume with a brief discussion of one of the principal blocks to understanding, Montherlant's penchant for auto-criticism. Such reëxamination of the author's intent is necessary for an understanding of his works. In harmony with his request that his works be seen as entities apart from his personal life, I have rarely attempted, except in my treatment of the lyric period, to intermingle autobiography with my study of his literary production; I am convinced that his literary production can only be understood by itself and not as an outcropping of a lifelong diary or even as a precise expression of personal experience.

The complete works of Montherlant are so extensive that I have restricted the scope of this volume to a study of his major production, omitting publications in limited editions.[1] I have also eliminated from close examination his many essays—except "Syncrétisme et alternance" in *Aux fontaines du désir*—that lie on the periphery of his creativity, especially since they repeat the sense of his major works. Most of his essays, often masterpieces of brilliant style, are essentially personal reminiscences or else brief documents written for specific occasions. They, together with the *Carnets*,[2] are marginal commentaries or polemic literature that stand apart from his fiction and drama. I have also omitted from my discussion *L'Histoire de "La Rose de sable,"* a fragment of an unpublished novel; *Pasiphaé* because of its incompleteness as a drama; and the poetry of the lyric period, especially in *Encore un instant de bonheur*, since Montherlant's best poetry is contained in his mature prose works.

I should like, finally, to express my appreciation to my wife for her examination of the manuscript and for her valuable suggestions in its preparation.

ROBERT B. JOHNSON

University of Massachusetts
Amherst, Massachusetts

Acknowledgment

I am particularly grateful to Editions Gallimard for its kind and generous permission to quote from the works of Henry de Montherlant.

Contents

Chronology

1896 Montherlant born in Paris, April 21. Son of Joseph Millon de Montherlant and Marguerite Camusat de Riancey.

1904 First attempts at writing; penchant for composing notes and commentaries.

1905–1907 Student at the Lycée Janson-de-Sailly, 1905–1906; private tutoring by priests. 1906–1907; friendship with Faure-Biguet.

1907 Student, until 1910, at the Ecole Saint-Pierre.

1908 Writing, in collaboration with Faure-Biguet.

1911 Student, from January, at the Ecole Sainte-Croix de Neuilly. First experience in killing bulls during vacation in Spain.

1912 Dismissal, in March, from the Ecole Sainte-Croix. Passes Baccalauréat examinations and begins law studies at the Institut Catholique, in Paris.

1913 Fails law examination. Period devoted to sports.

1914 Death of father. Writes *L'Exil.*

1915 Death of mother.

1916–1919 Military experiences (in auxiliary service); wounded in 1918; interpreter with American forces from 1919. Begins *Le Songe.*

1920 Publication (at his expense) of *La Relève du matin.*

1921 Active participation in sports until 1924.

1922 Publication of *Le Songe.*

1924 Publication of *Les Olympiques* and *Chant funèbre pour les morts de Verdun.*

1925 Begins period of wandering which lasts until 1935. Further experiences in the bullring.

1926 Publication of *Les Bestiaires.* Travels in Africa.

1927 Publication of *Aux fontaines du désir.*

1928 Writes *Pasiphaé* and *Chant de Minos,* fragments of his unpublished *Les Crétois.*

1929 Publication of *L'Exil* and of *La Petite Infante de Castille.*

1932 Publication of *Mors et vita.*

1934 Publication of *Encore un instant de bonheur;* publication of *Les Célibataires,* which earns for him the English Northcliffe-Heineman Prize for Literature and the French Academy's Grand Prix de Littérature.

1935 Publication of *Service inutile.*

1936 Publication of the first two novels of *Les Jeunes Filles: Les Jeunes Filles* and *Pitié pour les femmes.* Publication of *Pasiphaé.*

1937 Publication of *Le Démon du bien* (third novel of *Les Jeunes Filles*).

1938 Publication of *L'Equinoxe de septembre.*

1939 Publication of *Les Lépreuses* (fourth and last novel of *Les Jeunes Filles*).

1940 Residence in the south of France after the German occupation.

1941 Return to Paris. Publication of *Le Solstice de juin.* Periods of residence in Grasse.

1942 Publication of *La Reine morte;* presented at the Comédie Française.

1943 Performance of *Fils de personne* at the Théâtre Saint-Georges; play published in 1944 with *Un Incompris.*

1945 Publication of *Un Voyageur solitaire est un diable.*

1946 Publication of *Malatesta;* first performed in 1950 at the Théâtre Marigny (Compagnie Madeleine Renaud-Jean-Louis Barrault).

1947 Publication of *Le Maître de Santiago;* first performed in 1948 at the Théâtre-Hébertot.

1949 Publication of *Demain il fera jour;* first performed in the Théâtre-Hébertot, together with *Fils de personne.*

1950 Publication of *Celles qu'on prend dans ses bras;* first performance at the Théâtre de la Madeleine.

1951 Publication of *La Ville dont le prince est un enfant;* Montherlant refuses to permit the play's performance except by amateurs.

1953 Publication of *Textes sous une occupation. Pasiphaé* performed at the Comédie Française; *Fils de personne* added to repertory of Comédie Française.

1954 Publication of *L'Histoire d'amour de "La Rose de sable,"* a fragment of the unpublished *La Rose de sable.* Publication of *Port-Royal;* first performed at the Comédie Française.

1956 Publication of *Brocéliande;* performance at the Comédie Française.
1957 Publication of *Carnets* (*1930–1944*) as single collection.
1958 Performance of *Le Maître de Santiago* at the Comédie Française. Publication of *Don Juan;* first performance at the Théâtre de l'Athénée.
1960 Publication of *Le Cardinal d'Espagne.*
1963 Publication of *Le Chaos et la nuit.* Election to the Académie Française.
1965 Publication of *La Guerre civile.*
1966 Publication of *Va jouer avec cette poussière* (*Carnets 1958–1964*).

CHAPTER 1

Enigma and Controversy

I *An Author Not of His Time*

MONTHERLANT is French literature's twentieth century maverick. Of course, France's literary élite is endowed with an ingrained sense of logic hopefully directed to understanding only the logical, and it is enamored of literary categories that should be measurable, rational, and functional. It is not altogether surprising that a writer who strikes out on his own to create and enrich his own unique art, one quite separate from the categories of the literary "establishment," risks a wide condemnation through inevitable misunderstanding; and yet the maverick author may attain his ultimate victory even if, as Montherlant wryly notes, such a victory is posthumous. To observe the work of Montherlant at the present time does pose the problem of focus. Such close observation, however, is needed to counteract the ultra-conservatism of French critics amazingly alarmed at anything new or different on the horizon. Despite its conservatism, France has long served as the catalyst in many areas of art—too late on occasion, if we recall only the "Americanization" of the Impressionists. Similarly, several centuries were needed to unfetter France's seventeenth century classicism; poetic technique successfully freed itself only in the second half of the nineteenth century, although a few arch-conservatives still deny the masterpieces of a Mallarmé or a Rimbaud even now in the mid-point of our century. Certainly, a few artists and whole movements of ideas—Existentialism and the so-called New Novel, for example—still lack full judgment at a moment when new trends in literature are already taking their places.

Montherlant's rôle as writer is indeed bizarre if judged in the light of recent past and current conservatism. To a certain degree he has solved his own problem by vociferously denying the sense of any literary judgment, especially when it emanates from the literary élite; like Rimbaud, prankishly engulfed in his own hermetic world, Montherlant chains his creative process in a secretive private world he chooses not to divulge, at least during his lifetime. What he does reveal is a vastly orchestrated composite of many elements: the self and others as seen by the self, life as experienced by the self, and life as observed by the self. He claims that his work reflects an utter simplicity and the essence of life because he concerns himself with truth. But it is he who insists upon explaining himself and his work to his public, especially in the measured doses of his countless notes, and he refuses to acknowledge opinion forever seeking Montherlant behind the work or devising novel concepts within it. He is an ardent enemy of hypotheses.

By rights, Montherlant's background should have placed him on a par with his judges, and he should long ago have expressed a conservatism to match theirs. Born amidst the Tout-Paris, well trained academically, although not obligated financially to pursue law studies, he chose to deny his social class as unworthy of emulation, to deny his Catholic faith out of clear conviction, and to question the values of his society and nation. Released from family "bondage" by the deaths of his parents and finally of his grandmother, he sought to become, especially after 1925, someone quite unlike either his family or the Tout-Paris. In becoming a new being—his work demonstrates to what degree the evolution was a slow process—he became more and more incomprehensible to those of his milieu, as well as an enemy to critics examining his literary production. But in becoming himself he renounced everything that his milieu signified. A singular lack of comprehension still exists today, for his continued resistance against conformity at all levels has led to a bitterness expressed now and again in his work, seconded by an equal bitterness voiced by a negative criticism. Symbolic of his curiously independent stance was his refusal to conform to all of the archaic ritual—suggestive of humility and submissiveness—that the candidate for the French Academy must go through before final election; his refusal to abide by the rules, as well as his election, appalling perhaps to the conservatives of the literary world, represented a personal victory that must still give Montherlant some pleasure.[1]

The truth of the matter is that Montherlant cannot be placed logically in predetermined, or even in new, categories that critics may devise for him. Except for his novelette *L'Histoire d'amour de "La Rose de sable,"* with its Flaubertian turns of phrase, or for

Les Célibataires, which has the undeniable ring of Balzac, his works stand far apart from the many literary movements of the nineteenth century; he plays no rôle whatsoever in the movements of the twentieth century, whether literary or philosophical. Many critics, in their often serious determination to find labels of convenience, attempt valiantly to shove his works into patterns, especially into pre-established patterns that are instantly recognizable. Because of *Malatesta,* his drama of the Italian Renaissance, Montherlant becomes somehow a man of the Renaissance, especially since Faure-Biguet's publication of *Montherlant, homme de la Renaissance* and Datain's *Montherlant et l'héritage de la Renaissance.*[2] Inevitably the question arises: Is Malatesta a Montherlant in Renaissance clothing? Certainly, a perusal of some essays and the *Carnets* brings out rather rapidly such a possibility. Again, in the *Carnets* as in the essays one finds also Montherlant the *moraliste,* and by way of a strange metamorphosis he becomes another Saint-Simon passing judgment on a society and an era; to add to the confusion is the knowledge that Montherlant admires Saint-Simon.[3] He is also a modern La Rochefoucauld, of course, quick to sharpen a maxim leveled at his contemporaries, or better, at the world in which his contemporaries move. I do not think it far-fetched to note, although perhaps with the aid of literary surgery, the flavor of Molière—I am thinking of *Brocéliande* rather than *Don Juan*—or at least the flavor of the Libertines of the seventeenth century. While he is in a restricted sense a "man of the Renaissance" and of the "Classic Age," Montherlant is also a fervent "Roman," and he seems to sustain the quality of Rome's brutalizing influence throughout his works: yet only one play, *La Guerre civile,* is specifically devoted to Roman history. In brief, Montherlant belongs to no specific age, and he fits into no precise categories.

Whether Montherlant's "Romanization" stems from his early reading of *Quo vadis?* is beside the point: his Rome springs from his own imagination and is supported by a knowledge of Roman history that he has romanticized. By the same token, Montherlant's Spain is precisely a Montherlantian Spain. It is never the Spain of history or the Spain of literature and guidebooks, but rather the latter days of the best of Rome in evolution as seen through the eyes of a Romantic. Spain and Rome are not the farthest reaches of Montherlant's imagination, for behind those cultures lie the legendary worlds of Persia, of Crete, and of all the pre-Christian Mediterranean civilizations so often at the root of his writing.

If Montherlant's work is inspired by a multiplicity of Mediterranean worlds, beginning with the pagan and ending with the Christian, it is important to underline its essentially pagan aura, despite a *Port-Royal,* a *Maître de Santiago,* or a *Cardinal d'Espagne.* In his work God appears to be in total confusion. The reader of these plays will sense a religious atmosphere at once serious and profound. But the total work of Montherlant is filled with the powers of pagan gods. It is essentially godless, despite titles, situations, rich vestments, and the dialogue of Christian faith. I believe him whenever he claims years of alienation from Catholicism and from any Christian faith. Of course, it is always tempting and comfortable to provide an author with religious views and to clothe him in acceptibility; such a task is made easier if there is a *Port-Royal* to justify an author's apparent Christianity, or to push on toward the grand label of Jansenism, a label now become highly respectable in the world of letters.[4]

But in somewhat the same context, critics of recent date tend to accept his godlessness for what it is, while moving toward a more interesting extension of that godlessness. They find that Montherlant is an existentialist. Indeed, there are traces of Existentialism in his work: nihilism, although frequently balanced by a salvation of meaningful action. While suicide—the better word is renunciation—is a recurring theme in his writings, it is less a planned attempt to quit life than an unplanned death wish. It is a short step from Montherlant as "existentialist" to Montherlant the self-torturer. But in balance with his concern for life's bleakness is still that other concern, his love of freedom; yet it is a freedom never realized.[5]

What is disturbing, of course, is the fact that there is an element of truth in almost everything serious that has been written about Montherlant, and the enigma of his lengthy work—if there is a real enigma—arises from a general unwillingness to absorb the many facets of his writing and to make them fit into a unity free of labels. It is true that the unity of his works becomes clear only after an examination of the whole. T. S. Eliot has remarked that the French, unlike the English and Americans, possess the common sense of searching for meaning and beauty in an author's total *oeuvre;* such comprehensive study does result in a full understanding of the author's merit, of his purpose and of his quality of expression. A study of single works, on the other hand, usually results in inaccurate hypotheses: Montherlant's *Don Juan,* for example, might well ruin his dramatic career were it the only play available for comment. *Port-Royal,* read out of the context of the other plays, might well establish the Catholic-Jansenist bent of the author, but such a reading could scarcely explain the pagan vitality of *Malatesta* or the somber politics of *La Guerre civile.*

A further reason for calling Montherlant an enigma is his unwillingness to clarify—that is, to clarify without reservations—the sense of his works; he refuses in a very real sense to "play the game" with his public and especially with his critics. To be sure, he is firmly convinced that his own clarifications, expressed many times in his multitudinous notes and in his *Carnets,* are entirely sufficient for both public and critics. But two problems confront students of Montherlant. First, his reservations—that portion of his thought he refuses to divulge—prevent clarity of vision. Second, Montherlant often fails to see the lack of logic in some of his own conclusions offered in both essays and notes; since he is endowed with a vivid imagination, he often sees more in his work than there is to be seen. The creative mind cannot always stop functioning with the final period of a novel or the last drop of a stage curtain. He admits, moreover, to a love for covering up the traces of his own design, and he therefore obfuscates intentionally the precise sense he may have originally wanted to offer his public. However, I believe that we really have no quarrel with Montherlant concerning the issue of clarity: "playing the game" in the sense I have described is a dishonest procedure in Montherlant's view; at least he is quite clear in his intention to muddy his traces, to be inventive, and to weave autobiographical threads into his works to such an extent that the threads form new patterns. But many readers find his obfuscation too deliberate and sometimes a little coy. The alienation of many critics largely stems from their feeling that Montherlant cheats them or mindlessly leads them astray. Yet the public is also to blame for its wish for simplicity and order. It rarely objects to an author's secretive destruction of pathways—the pathways of his creative process—provided their destruction is not announced boldly, as is Montherlant's wont. Montherlant takes pride not simply in revealing several antinomies so often attributed to artists—the godly and the godless, for example—but he takes an even greater pride in divulging a multiplicity of characteristics, as stylist and as moralist, characteristics which he claims to be the multiple features of human beings. He views the human as the natural embodiment of an infinite many-sidedness in the psychological sense, precisely because he is human, and he rejects the narrowness of man's simplistic dualism and the impossibility of a single-featured man.

It is nevertheless true that a sensitive artist, constantly misunderstood by his impatient public, risks the danger of self-destruction. It is a form of "suicide" toward which the solitary artist often propels himself unthinkingly. Montherlant's sensitive reactions to his critics make him accept magnanimously into his camp those who find nothing but good in his work, and make him reject with surprising fury those who hesitate to accept its values. He wages a private (and public) war: a misstep of comprehension, a slight misinterpretation, or a gentle slap on the wrist for a lapse in esthetics, for example, can evoke a storm of protest from Montherlant—or else his absolute and unyielding silence. In his public addresses he needlessly rushes to the defense of his works as if they needed a defense years after their publication. He still seems strangely unaware of his merit. His critical amplifications often have the quality of desperation: he explicates his works before they become defenselessly posthumous. The creative artist wages constant war against the *clercs*—the "clerks" of criticism, to use his own term—who deform and defoliate art before the eyes of the creator.

Readers of his critics in both French and English may be surprised, therefore, to find two major judgments, neither of which may be very satisfying to the serious student. On the one hand, Montherlant is judged to be unworthy because he lacks sincerity: his works are nothing but a series of frames in which different masks of Montherlant appear willy-nilly to amuse or appall readers. On the other hand, his works are held up as supreme examples of literary grandeur in the twentieth century; it is a grandeur without shading. Of course, readers will have to discover a middle ground as vantage point to capture the many qualities, both good and bad, of his literary production. Such critical battles are normal, especially in France where opinions are freely expressed rather than repressed. At least, Montherlant's rush toward a figurative self-destruction as a somewhat violent defender of his art will in no way destroy his art. Time will assuage the exaggerations of conservative criticism and ultimately bring together into a digestible whole the many divergent opinions that now tend to confuse: a solid portion of his work will endure. And why not accept Montherlant as an enigma? There must be an enigmatic strain in a work called poetry by its creator.

II *At the Root of Montherlant's Works: The "Universal Man"*

I am not sure to what extent Montherlant is aware of the appropriateness and poetic implication of his early key essay, "Syncrétisme et alternance." [6] The term "syncretism," derived from the Greek word *synkretismos,* denoting a federation of Cretan cities, has the power to recall instantly Montherlant's intense devotion to ancient Crete, to the pagan bestiality of a Minos and the sensuous world of a Minotaur and a Pasiphaë; the word evokes the whole rich tapestry of images that have become Montherlant's own in works that re-deify the island's past. Yet the essay does not underline his awareness of the word's root meaning, and I believe it to be only a fortuitous choice on his part.

What is striking is the early date of the brief essay—1925.[7] By rights, it should somehow bear a much more recent date, for "Syncrétisme et alternance" is directly related to all of the major ideas developed over a long career; it is undoubtedly the *sine qua non* for those who intend to reach the sense of his entire work. While Montherlant sometimes persuades us that certain early essays—those of *La Relève du matin,* for example—reflect rather dimly in retrospect the views of the mature writer, he cannot deny the unchanging quality of the thoughts set forth in the root essay; those thoughts, stated with utter simplicity and clarity, are found mirrored even in his latest works. It must be stated at once that Montherlant does not constantly change, reversing his opinions, his attitudes, and beliefs, moving on to newer worlds of his own creation. On the contrary, he possesses a static core of thought capable of many manifestations; he has always been able, however, to orchestrate such manifestations, always on a grand scale, but without altering the central core. The center of his entire reasoning and thought is established in "Syncrétisme et alternance."

The essay is not a pleasant one to read. It opens to public view the wounds of human weakness without offering at the same time the esthetic veneer of civilization. It displays the godless human. But I have imposed the terms "wounds" and "weakness," which are scarcely Montherlantian: they are rather the comfortable words our society may assign to the uncomfortable human condition in some effort to discuss it pleasantly. Montherlant's godless or amoral human is depicted with complete honesty, and such honesty repels, at least in certain milieus. The human animal under such close scrutiny may become clinical in scope, and he may be rejected as too alien to the true human condition, whatever that may be. But this is a century that has tried in one way or another to determine the meaning of man's humanity. The problem of man's failure still raises unanswerable questions.

While Montherlant is neither an existentialist nor a philosopher, he does undertake the study of the human condition as he understands it, and he often sees the absurdity of man. But for Montherlant the absurd is not a surprising portion of human existence; it is rather a natural phenomenon. We create such a term to explain away the irrational idiocies of man in his environment. Montherlant holds that all facets of the human, whether base animal or highly developed creature, are true and hence worthy of close examination. Man is not one thing or another, however: he is all things mixed together in a common blend. Today's animalistic creature is tomorrow's intellectual, or today's mask can become tomorrow's face. Hence, the term "absurd" is quite meaningless in terms of a Montherlantian psychology which rejects all notions of a high intellectualism from which the term springs. His animal-man is far closer to the primitive state than to a civilized one, and what tends to confuse his readers is the constant necessity of viewing his human creations as essentially animalistic. Standing in the way is Montherlant's intellectual, heroic language that clothes the animalistic in fine array; the reader must be prepared to penetrate the wall of language to understand syncretic man.

I have stated that "Syncrétisme et alternance" is not a comfortable essay to read because of its stark honesty. Montherlant's point of departure is the study of the human animal in answer to Romain Rolland's *Au-dessus de la mêlée*. He accomplishes his task not by underlining a dual nature in man, but rather by underlining a single quality inherent in man's nature, a quality capable of infinite expansion and expression. War, for example, elicits man's passions on several levels—patriotism, sacrifice, xenophobia, instinct for battle and for killing, to use Montherlant's own terms—and these passions are normal "fruits of our entrails." [8] Just how far removed from reality is Montherlant? Is he overstating the case, especially with reference to base passions? Of course, psychologists are able to explain the reasons for man's patriotism, especially of a patriotism born in wartime: certainly, collective security and a feeling of oneness are at the heart of the matter, together with the greater passion for staying alive. Sacrifice is always a direct product of war and is often motivated by custom and necessity. Xenophobia, a normal condition of man, becomes in wars suddenly just and rational. At an overly intellectual level, to be sure, patriotism would lose its urgent force, sacrifice would become more meaningless, and xenophobia would simply be a state of mind best held in check. As for the instinct for battle, which Montherlant joins to the other common passions of war, psychologists do relate the animalistic baseness of the human animal, and they compare him with a cannibalistic pack of rats; it has been demonstrated that even wolves have a "code of decency" with respect to killing their own kind. Rational man, of course, is not the base creature Montherlant describes; yet Montherlant does grasp an understanding of man's horrendous capacity for destruction. "Moral" man, given certain positive checks imposed by church, laws, and simply the wish to exist, stands at the edge of chaos. Deploring the chaos, man still strives to elevate himself—and hopefully, perhaps egotistically, to elevate his fellow beings as well. Yet Montherlant's man is somewhat removed from any ennobling, brake-like, morality. Montherlant is particularly aware of the appalling dishonesty of states engaged in warfare: such states always proclaim their devotion to high moral purposes, and they all pray for divine help, often to the same God.

Montherlant agrees that Romain Rolland's Germany of Goethe and Attila the Hun is not a paradox. The poet and heathen can exist together in the same national psychology without seeming to be out of harmony. Both Goethe and Attila—as symbols of man's contrary nature—represent in reality multiple manifestations of human possibility: "Goethe and Attila emanate from a single source of universal energy. Phenomena of nature, they are bound together." [9] At the core of man lies the Goethe-Attila essence, but I rather think that Montherlant finds the honesty of the primitive Attila more immediately attractive than the culture of Goethe—whom he occasionally admires. It is Montherlant's curious conclusion to his statement that gives us a portion of the key to understanding his work. The beauty and grandeur of the universe arise from both the good and evil that are in it, and Goethe and Attila are symbols of good and evil. He adds: "Let us fight against Attila, but while remaining aware of his superior usefulness; let us fight against him with deep complaisance and, to sum up, let us fight against him while esteeming him." [10] Montherlant's view of the higher utility of an Attila, or his strange suggestion that we must do battle with Attila while esteeming him, stems from his firm belief that a love for battle and an esteem for the enemy are portions of the universal truth of man's condition. Man ought therefore to embrace with naturalness all facets of such truth. There is nothing in life to convince man that warfare need be shorn of symbolic "love." Hatred, not to be rejected from this natural universe, has its special value—particularly when added to power and ambition—that derives only from justifiable application. "I continue to believe," Montherlant writes in his essay, "that to be human is to understand all the movements of man." [11]

But man, according to Montherlant, is not reduced to a common inferior condition because he is thus multifaceted. His grandeur is his intelligent—but not necessarily intellectual—comprehension that the whole human condition is unbelievably multiplied according to the possibilities of the brain's scope. Right and wrong, or morality at any level of understanding and acceptability, are replaced by right and right: the idea of evil and the sense of wrongness do not make sense. Readers will remember the Pascalian maxim that makes of man neither beast nor angel, although Montherlant is remarkably far removed from a Pascalian, or Jansenist, morality.[12] Montherlant does create a truth out of a paradox: "To be at once, or rather to have alternate within the self, Beast and Angel, corporal and carnal life with moral and intellectual life, will be forced upon man, willing or not, by nature which is totally composed of alternations, contradictions, and détentes." [13] And he states what serves as a motto for his entire work: "We see that *everything is true.*" [14] If everything is true, then it reasonably follows that everything is possible, save for obstacles imposed physically or by some non-universal code of morality. Montherlant admits the poetic possibilities of man shorn of morality—amoral man—of man aware of the universal sense of truth lying behind all human motivation: "Violence, superstitions, discretions, all instincts, all ecstasies, the entire perfumed drove of passions—that my logic and moral conscience reject—return secretly to their proper order, called back by my poetry." [15] To be a writer, hence a creative artist—the term "poet" is his own and he uses it to describe himself—Montherlant must be unfettered: "I am a poet and just that, and I need to love and to experience the world's diversities and all of its supposed opposites, because they are at the root of my poetry, which would die of starvation in a universe governed only by truth and right, just as we would die of thirst if we were to drink only chemically pure water." [16]

Montherlant's sense of liberty—some may wish to call it rather his sense of libertinage—is unrestricted. In this early lyric essay he admits to an affinity for the unusual in nature: animals, plants, women, all living beings are drawn to his own nature by sensual-sexual bonds whose rejection would constitute for him a rejection of the natural universe. But his links with natural phenomena are not to be accepted willy-nilly as a sort of growing "baggage" that could one day prove troublesome. Central to his thinking is the necessity of accepting and the necessity of rejecting; there must always be a constant renewal, for sameness is in a large sense a rejection of nature. Montherlant anticipates his public's misinterpretation of his concept of a "universal law": it does not embrace the idea of a vast love affair with nature, although love as a temporary sensuous experience is not excluded. His antidote for love—a love that must never be cloying, possessive, or even profound—is indifference. Indeed, indifference is a word that appears with regularity in his entire work. While always lying at the opposite end of Montherlant's scale of values, in balance with love, indifference has the same value in his natural universe; I believe that indifference all but replaces love in his later works. It recurs as a sort of negative virtue, a portion of the nihilism explicit in his works. Since his concept of love is not profound, his adherence to indifference is entirely believable.

III *The Mystique of Rome*

Montherlant's alternating, syncretic man has changed little since 1925. Despite the possible implications of the terms—the possibility of poetic vagueness, for example—they explain the unity of his work. The pagan Montherlant has never removed himself from the pagan world of Crete. But a larger world, brutal and brutalizing, of romanticized Rome has more often drawn his attention. To some measurable degree the gentler civilization of Greece appears in his work: *Les Olympiques* smacks rather of his brief encounter with Greece, but the work is essentially "Romanized," despite an intensely lyric quality. His dramatic poem *Pasiphaé* and his major poetry collection *Encore un instant de bonheur* have a Cretan-Roman stamp. It is Rome—the Montherlantian vision of a Rome that never existed—that explains the lyric *Le Songe;* Roman *dominio,* the need to dominate, explains the often curious attitudes he has toward an enemy, toward friends, toward situations, and even toward himself. Again, his discovery of Spain is less a love affair with a modern European culture than a discovery of a reincarnation of his Roman world. In *Les Bestiaires* he is rarely concerned with the contemporary but is almost always enamored of the Spanish traits that (he thinks) Rome evokes: *dominio* is his word-symbol used to describe the Spanish extension of Rome's use of force to dominate. His personal and literary fascination for bullfighting stems from the concept of *dominio:* power over an animal.[17]

We are then not concerned with genuineness—with an authentic Rome or an authentic Spain—but rather with a mystique. Of course, it is his right as a poet to create new visions of ancient cultures, even if his visions fall far short of their mark in terms of reality. I doubt, for example, that Spaniards find themselves accurately reflected in Montherlant's works. On the other hand, they may recognize, if in a poetic sense, the essence of his mystique of Rome as applied to them. Sports are also a part of the same vast mystique, of course: it is not correct to assume now that Montherlant is less interested in them because he no longer actively participates in them. Similarly, he is no less an aficionado of the bullring today than he was as a boy: his recent play, *Le Cardinal d'Espagne,* is designed—although perhaps in retrospect—to follow the dramatic movements of the corrida.[18] Finally, by analogy, Renaissance Italy is in balance with Montherlant's Spain, for certainly *Malatesta* is a clear portion of the mystique of Rome. Even *La Reine morte,* whose action takes place in Portugal, is not distant from a poetic Spain or a poetic Renaissance Italy. It is rather a simple matter to see the Romanization of Ferrante (in *La Reine morte*), but it is made clearer in the hero of *Malatesta* or in Cisneros of *Le Cardinal d'Espagne.* It is not unrealistic to observe the identical mystique in the dramatic scope of his plays of contemporary theme. In *Fils de personne* and *Demain il fera jour,* for example, there is the familiar ring of Rome, the same treatment of sacrifice and indifference, the rejection of mediocrity and the glorification of power.

The Romanization, as mystique, is indeed well established in all facets of Montherlant's works. Since it is a mystique, it is pointless to search for the real Rome. His ancient Latin world is heavily laden with Romanticism; it is his own creation. It is no more fictitious in one sense than *Quo vadis?*, a novel well known to Montherlant since his childhood, for the novel also expresses a Christian-pagan mystique of its own. It would be a mistake to insist that Montherlant's mystique repeats that of the novel, for his is under the influence of "Syncrétisme et alternance."

I find a rather natural phenomenon that may explain the curious psychology of his literary figures: they are the direct opposites of everyone moving in Montherlant's Parisian milieu. A son of the Tout-Paris, he was overly protected, often isolated, from the hardships and the brutality of normal existence; his was a life in a hothouse. Well-off financially, Montherlant has never met acute hardships at a material level, nor has he been forced to compete with his peers. At first protected from society, Montherlant later chose to alienate himself from it precisely at the time he discovered that other world of ancient Mediterranean cultures.[19] He rejected the mediocre and the banal at an early age in order to seek an identity in worlds that never really existed. This form of escapism—often to try to find forbidden fruits—is far more normal in life and literature than one might suppose. I am not convinced that his invented worlds have made him content personally: man's distress is frequently portrayed in his works. We are dealing with a poet who is free to create an imagery of his own devising and free to reveal the self without defining the self; he can build temples of sensuality where blood used to flow. We should never expect Montherlant to be authentic: Rome's virtues outweigh its crimes against humanity, a fact which he chooses not to discuss. The facts of Roman civilization are without importance for him; he is rarely concerned with the government of Rome. He is aware of Rome's social stratification, with slavery at the bottom; Montherlant, of course, would have been a citizen of Rome.

Montherlant's Roman mystique is singularly one-sided and obstinate; it is equally one-sided when it becomes a Spanish or an Italian mystique—although they are all the same. His Romanticism is really an acute sensitivity to the sensual life of the past. It is well to avoid calling Montherlant a modern Roman, which he is not at all, but rather a modern Romantic imbued with the mystique of Rome. We should never expect this poet to become the historian of Classicism, even when he calls upon history for justification of details. He alters history slightly to create a *Port-Royal* or a *Cardinal d'Espagne* in order to examine the humans of history. Despite his changes, and especially despite his constant imposition of the self in extended dialogues, his historicity emerges with great art. His best works contain three major values: first, his focus on the nature of man is true; second, he catches the sense of history; and finally, he blends them with poetry that emanates from his vast mystique.

IV *The Solitary Hero*

As a poet, of course, Montherlant is not going to perform as we would like him to perform. He displays throughout his works his vision of man as described in "Syncrétisme et alternance," a man created out of the author's imagination. Montherlant superimposes visions upon visions, situations upon situations, swerves deftly from ecstasy to acrimony, and he changes facades with the same ease as he changes genres. Beneath the elaborations of his compositions of alternation there always stands the same human animal. Montherlant would have us believe that such a human is all of us reduced to simple and honest terms. What is surprising is the accuracy of his portrayal; despite elaborations, his human animal emerges as a familiar being we can recognize.

I have already underlined the essential unity of Montherlant's works: universal man, syncretic and alternating. His heroes—or non-heroes, depending upon the work—also have their unity shaped by the mystique of Rome: they are elaborations of the human animal. His hero prototype is something less than Caesar, and he is often a reflection of Hamlet. In their attempt to see Montherlant in each hero too many readers fail to realize that his heroes are weak and inhibited, unable to act; they are often far from heroic. The Montherlantian hero is a sensitive and sensual creature existing in an alien environment (alien because it is ignoble); he is in constant struggle with himself and is inevitably doomed to destruction. He is not an unworldly Caesar devoid of shading, but rather a man of all times. Montherlant's hero is completely human: he risks defeat brought about by his own weaknesses rather than a defeat inflicted by others, who are not always his equals.[20] Without faith—faith is of last importance even in his Catholic dramas—the hero must look inward upon himself and act in solitary combat, or else die in symbolic suicide. The hero who struggles against his fate is a genuinely tragic hero; the hero who does not, or cannot, act, like Léon de Coantré of *Les Célibataires,* is certainly tragic—but he is a non-hero. There is a curious

Janus-like quality about the Montherlantian hero: although always the same human animal, he can be either hero or non-hero depending on the author's immediate purpose. Turn the bust of Léon de Coantré a half-circle and one finds a Malatesta; both Léon and Malatesta are examples of Montherlant's universal man.

At the root of Montherlantian tragedy is the hero's inability to accept human weaknesses in others. The reader is struck by the sameness of the stamp of rejection of others whether he reads *L'Exil* or *La Guerre civile*. First, there is a rejection of love and sympathy as we think we understand these terms; sentimentality plays no rôle in his work. His heroes do not display forms of affection. Non-sentimental love, hence purely sensual, flows in to fill the vacuum of hate, and hate flows in to fill the vacuum of love: this is the essential movement of Montherlantian psychology. Second, *dominio,* or mastery of another's body and soul, lies at the root of action; without *dominio*—Léon de Coantré, for example—the hero is in a sort of limbo. If he possesses it, like Malatesta, he holds on to humanity. For the hero who possesses *dominio* there is little room for sympathy or for charity, although Montherlant insists upon using such terms—especially charity—in a meaningless way. More important is the knowledge that *dominio* is always a state of human relationship to be achieved, hence an ideal; yet it is rarely achieved in his works. The other people of the hero's world are usually too obtuse, too obstinate, and certainly too unworthy to master; worthy opponents such as the Attilas are hard to find. In this context I should like to underline the insidious isolation of the Montherlantian hero who never attains fulfillment, rarely knows poetic ecstasy, and usually meets a bleak and meaningless death.

The minor characters of Montherlant's works are entirely minor by contrast with the hero. In a very real sense Montherlant creates a central figure who elucidates his own state of self—his *état d'âme,* to use a more precise expression—and all or most of the other characters are mirror-images of the single central figure. It is possible to note a further dramatic effect: the work of Montherlant is composed essentially of monologues spoken by the hero. The sense of the monologues is clarified, made more dramatically intense, and enriched by other, minor monologues spoken by the lesser players. The method is the same for both novels and plays. *La Reine morte* is primarily a soliloquy of Ferrante, a soliloquy interrupted by the speeches of the other actors. In his novel *Le*

Chaos et la nuit, Celestino's dialogues are quite similar to dramatic soliloquies; they are interrupted by dialogues of the minor characters as well as by the author's narrative embellishments. Montherlant's narrations should properly be called elucidations rather than simple expositions. In this context it is perhaps well to mention that some critics find Montherlant entirely too verbose, especially in his plays, and it is true that they are often cut. The soliloquy does require a disciplined hand: Montherlant's clarifications in context, coupled with infrequent non sequiturs, do extend at times beyond the limits of need. I attribute such extensions to his enthusiasm and to a sincere wish to be totally clear. The impatient reader or audience cannot come to grips with Montherlant's works.

V *Montherlant and Women*

The women of Montherlant's works, most closely studied in *Les Jeunes Filles,* have aroused wide controversy; they are absent only from his latest play, *La Guerre civile.* The four novels of the tetralogy, *Les Jeunes Filles,* seem to assure his rôle as contemporary literature's supreme misogynist, but I think it is time to cast a more careful glance at the problem. Of course, the concept of *dominio* found in all of his works tends to persuade many—especially Simone de Beauvoir—that by contrast with the hero all of Montherlant's women are weak, ineffectual creatures; they are objects rather than humans. To the contrary, however, women are never denied their normal position in his works, and the author does not deny them their humanity. But Montherlant's women must be entirely feminine to be admirable and admired; they are objects of man's love (sensuality) and they must play their natural rôles as mothers, wives, or friends. They must be all of these things without imposing an unnatural will to dominate or smother, and more important, they must avoid sentimentality at all cost. What sometimes confuses readers is his double attitude toward women who exert some form of power over men. He admires the grandeur of the Infanta of Navarre in *La Reine morte,* although she displays an obvious male *dominio;* but she is only a mirror-image of Ferrante and she does nothing to lessen Ferrante's own grandeur. Inés de Castro (of *La Reine morte*), on the other hand, is a pale, unassuming woman, but her sentimentality poses an obstacle. Inés is not killed because she is a woman—hence a victim, so to speak, of the author's misogyny—but rather because her death is a symbolic instrument of Ferrante's power: her rôle in the play is minor because her main rôle, as Pedro's wife and as mother-to-be, has already been played before the first act curtain rises. Inés exists in the drama; the Infanta as second image of Ferrante is a contrapuntal element.

Port-Royal, a drama devoted to the trials of cloistered nuns, poses a special problem of interpretation; misogyny is scarcely an issue. If all the sisters possessed the same passive nature visible in Inés de Castro, there would scarcely be a play worth following. If *dominio* is symbolically present in Church authority, it also exists among the nuns, each of whom displays a remarkably different personality. Some are feminine and passive, but others have a supreme strength—an almost sexless strength in the context of the play. While the Archbishop imposes his *dominio,* the sisters also have theirs as they play out the drama of devotion, sacrifice, and treason. Nowhere does Montherlant offer us a negative character simply because she is a woman: he has written a drama about treason and not a play about the treachery of women.

On the surface his four novels, *Les Jeunes Filles,* seem to study anti-feminism or at least an anti-feminine mystique. Yet it is clear from the outset that he undertakes to treat only certain types of women rather than all women. Montherlant regrets today that the novels have too many general statements. The novels relate the affairs of a writer, Costals, who attracts women precisely because he is an artist. Costals in none of the four novels is portrayed as having a special grandeur: he is distasteful and ludicrous. The women who are attracted to him, however, are quite another story. One woman, Thérèse Pantevin, who blends her psychopathic love-from-afar into her misguided religiosity, runs headlong toward self-destruction. Another, Andrée Hacquebaut, is incapable intellectually or emotionally of meeting Costals' world: she is a hopeless Romantic from the provinces, a bundle of mindless frustrations, with a scope so limited that only distance and correspondence link her to humanity. Actual confrontation with Costals is an agony. Of course, Costals takes delight in increasing her agony not because he dislikes women but rather because he is an honest animal: we are never far from the syncretic, alternating human. A third woman, Solange, poses a different problem because she more closely resembles the ideal, at least at the beginning. She suffers at the hands of Costals because he, like Ferrante, cannot completely dominate himself. He knows, for example, that his relationship with Solange will continue to be a strange dance of death because of his own weaknesses, which are more overwhelming than Solange's vague sentimentality. The reader can sympathize with a Thérèse and an Andrée without liking them, for they are too remote from reality. He can sympathize with a Solange subjected continuously to Costals' sadistic *dominio.* In *Les Jeunes Filles* Montherlant is not anti-feminine, and the novels themselves do not portray misogyny only because the women are bizarre and Costals is lost in private chaos.

It is beside the point to note that Costals is a writer, an intellectual. There is no evidence within the works that he is an intellectual of stature. He has a passion for isolation, but he is too human to separate himself completely from the world. Montherlant's attention is less often turned on the women than on the solitary Costals in the throes of personal defeat; he is concerned with describing the case history of one unheroic man affected by the dangers of a special milieu. The public's misunderstanding of the novels—justified in part by Montherlant's generalities—arise from the author's unfortunate habit of repeating episodes of the case history. I am inclined to believe that *Les Jeunes Filles* would have made a better single novel.

VI *Toward an Understanding*

I doubt that Montherlant and many of his critics will ever reach a comfortable truce during his lifetime unless his work continues to be reëxamined without the constant specter of the author. But then, Montherlant is not looking for comfort. He is a poet devoted to a highly personal mystique, and he displays a voice of strong intensity. During his lifetime, at least, some contemporaries will lash out at this maverick who dares to be different and who dares to choose a difficult isolation. They will call him a Costals—or an Alban-Don Juan or a Ferrante—in the hope that Montherlant the man will somehow explain the works and dissipate the hermetic quality they contain. It is far better to remember that after the lyric period he stands apart from his work. He has chosen a mystique instead of a philosophy; no historian, he has managed to lend an air of historic authenticity to many of his works. His studies of man, while never leading to precise clinical conclusions, should be valued as accurate insights into man's nature. To speak of his godliness or even of his Renaissance nature is to muddy the author's intentions and impose explications too far from the truth.

His strangely uncommon but accurate psychological view of universal man, shown to us with the amazingly precise instrument of a unique style, reveals the mind and method of the poet. It is necessary to shake off conventional concepts of genre in order to find at the core of his literary production the poetic insight.

CHAPTER 2

The Lyric Period

I *The Direction and the Definition of the Lyric Works*

IT is well to explain at the outset that the term "novel" is not altogether appropriate if we are to discuss the long prose works of Montherlant. Some works do reflect the accepted nineteenth century form of the genre, while others are unusually unique forms of the author's expression. Their plots are held together by slim threads, and they form what may be called "historiettes." [1] I am not at all surprised to discover Montherlant's unwillingness to adhere to a conservatism of form when his focus is elsewhere: style is his main instrument of expression. Ideas are not lacking in his early prose works, of course. As in his drama, he seeks with intellectual honesty to study man as he understands him, and his study reveals man impoverished and exposed to harsh light despite his veneer of civilization. From *Le Songe* (1922) to *Le Chaos et la nuit* (1963) Montherlant writes of man's condition and fate, although he remains on the periphery of the present century's concern with the same subject.

His novels reveal two major directions. His lyric works of the first period—*Le Songe, Les Olympiques, Les Bestiaires,* and *La Petite Infante de Castille*—defy classification.[2] But they can nonetheless be called poems in prose dedicated to the liberation of self searching for identity. True, it is possible to find in Montherlant's life an explanation of the lyric period. He was liberated from his family—especially from the restraints of his caste—at the age of twenty-nine; but he had already encountered his Mediterranean world, largely through reading, and Spain of the corridas in secretive experiences. He had long since rejected the values of his caste as well as his Catholic faith and begun to formulate the multifaceted human described in "Syncrétisme et alternance." [3] He became a sort of prodigal, but one who never returned completely satisfied to the fold—his Parisian milieu. In effect, he became the primitive pagan before leaving secondary school. Like Gide and others who have made a cult of North Africa, Montherlant discovered in Tangiers and elsewhere the keys to an identity; he preferred the simplicity of the Arabs to the society of Europeans. In Spain, too, he sought the company of the common man endowed with dignity and infinitely closer to human reality. In France, the *poilu,* the infantryman, replaced officialdom in his focus. And so *Les Bestiaires,* a novel devoted to aspects of the mystique of Rome, contains passages that show his hatred of caste, of foreigners, and of meaningless social obligations; foreigners frequently clutter his lyricism with their chaotic ineptitudes. The enemy of *Les Olympiques* is outlandish bourgeois stuffiness and especially parental mediocrity. The Infanta of Castille—that curious dancer who scarcely is traced in *La Petite Infante de Castille*—symbolizes primitivism and simplicity.

In throwing off the restraints of his caste, Montherlant has created a whole new set of problems. The primitivism he seeks, and in which he seems to find his genuine identity, is devoid of the intellectual. By means of his art Montherlant creates nevertheless an intellectualized primitivism—hence a false one outside of his own grasp. In a sense he creates for himself (and for his heroes) a false and impossible world which he can never enter, and in so doing he realizes a profound isolation. All of his works, even those of later periods, rather clearly demonstrate a failure to come to grips with the self: an intellectual imprisonment shows through to such a degree that his works constitute a literature of man's failure.

The early lyric works are a poetry of the primitive senses. He sets forth extremely accurate portrayals of sensual phenomena in a language of brilliant expression; it is perhaps unimportant that he never reaches "comfortable" conclusions. Because they are lyric songs of sensuality, they tend to lead unwary readers to be impatient with his conclusions, to be angry with his method, and to wonder at the sense of his subjects. The dilemma stems from the fact that his literary form persuades readers of a serious philosophic purpose which is unresolved. Secondly, Montherlant's constant preoccupation with human truths as he sees them often leads readers to deny the sense of his poetry. Again, the early works devoted to the mystique of Rome are devoid of Christianity even when they touch upon the subject.

Montherlant finds the true sense of man, and of manhood, in the Roman concept of *dignitas.* But he finds in pagan cultures more than *dignitas,* for he discovers the entire sense of simplicity as a human virtue, and it stands in his mystique as an opposition to caste. His Parisian society is understood to have an infinite assortment of false masks and focuses; it is unworthy, dishonest, ineffectual, boring, and in perpetual bondage to itself. One might expect Montherlant to have such a vision of his caste at an early age and to replace it with a more reasonable view as he matured. But despite his turn from a lyric direction in the early works, he remains unconvinced of the values of his family milieu; the pagan world still holds its impossible attractions. I have mentioned the impossibility of a marriage between true primitivism as he wishes it and the intellectualized primitivism as he creates it: it is undoubtedly this impossibility that in his later works brings about a tone of marked bitterness and sullen disapproval.

Montherlant has no faith, but he seems tied to a form of Catholicism, although he is drawn to it much as a man is drawn to admire a coat of arms: he esteems the symbols of Catholicism as they appear, for example, in *Les Bestiaires*. Without faith, he speaks of death as a "night," an ending of life's chaos, but he never discusses profoundly the significance of death. His works represent a pendulum swing in one direction—toward primitivism —with a return swing to (Christian) civilization; the ecstasies of life always exist in the single movement of the pendulum. Death is a normal termination. What he does underline in later works is a death-in-life through his study of renunciation, denial, perverse inaction. The title of his latest novel, *Le Chaos et la nuit*, serves to illustrate the changed Montherlant. In it he determines that life is a chaos through which man moves toward an inevitable end, death. At the other end of the scale is *Le Songe*, where life is described as a dream.

II Le Songe[4] (The Dream)

This disturbing first novel shows Montherlant in defiance of conformity. Ostensibly, *Le Songe* (1922) is devoted to World War I. Many readers have studied its chapters only in that light in an effort to understand the author's poetic interpretations of life and death, of the allied and enemy wounded, of love in wartime, and of war's futility. What the novel really represents is a vast, romanticized *culte du moi* on the part of the hero Alban de Bricoule. As for the revelations of the agonies of war, there is certainly little evidence that war itself plays a major rôle in the plot. War looms in the shadows, hidden for the most part by Montherlant's characters, and hangs in the background like some unchanging stage backdrop, drawing the reader's attention at the rare moments when the central characters are absent from the scene. I fail to see Montherlant's preoccupation with the horrors of war, with its pathetic realities or with its multiple hells. Today's sophisticated public refuses to accept any romanticization of battlefronts as intellectually bearable; we look with benign amusement even at a Winston Churchill dreaming in his latter days of that good war—the Boer Rebellion—where gentlemen conducted themselves as if they were in some sort of brilliantly disciplined chess game.

But World War I was for its generation a "romantic war," especially for the Allies who won it. Not curiously, the present television public in the United States finds a cuteness in the former enemy, especially in those amusing prison camps. Some twenty-five years after Pearl Harbor we are faced with a surprisingly popular array of programs devoted to actual combat. Of course, the memory plays tricks: for many, World Wars I and II meant a new freedom, a grasping at a new manhood, unforgettable associations, and certainly a sense of belonging; the brain rejects reality either because it wants to or never faced it. Similarly, the bloody murders in mystery stories hold no horror for their readers, for murders are merely the final portions of intellectual games we like to play. We must therefore excuse Montherlant for his treatment of World War I, for it was never his intention to show war's reality: his war is the stage on which facets of the mystique of Rome reveal themselves.

For Alban de Bricoule war is action—and action reposes.[5] He might have cried out: "Liberty in primitivism!" Alban's primitivism, a movement away fom Christian morality, persuades him of his need to participate always in a non-contemplative life. To convince himself of his urgent need for personal liberty, he declares a personal independence from all influence: *dominio* starts with the self.[6] The state of repose that Alban describes is not surprising if one remembers Anouilh's *Antigone,* in which the Chorus explains that tragedy itself is reposing and calming because it is clear-cut. For a time, Alban realizes that there is something to be done through action, but in the end, like the Chorus of *Antigone,* he knows there is nothing to do. Of course, Alban's strange sense of ecstatic freedom is monstrous. And Alban himself is monstrous throughout all of the episodes of *Le Songe* because, despite his expressions of his strength and dignity, he emerges as chaotic and weak. He is a youth alienated from society and utterly alone.

While war in *Le Songe* is unreal and therefore unmoving, the relationship between Alban and his friends is real and always in clear focus. Curiously his rapport with his mistress Douce, briefly mentioned in the novel, is largely impressionistic: she is the symbol of sensual primitivism but plays no direct part in *Le Songe.* Dominique Soubrier, a bright, athletic young woman, does play a major rôle. She is the literary "sister" of Solange in *Les Jeunes Filles.* Finally, Stanislas Prinet, Alban's friend at the front, closes the circle. They are bound together in a web of themes: renunciation, rejection, cruelty, sadism, all of which appear throughout Montherlant's works. The freedom Alban thinks he possesses feeds upon others for the very essence of nourishment, for his freedom, despite himself, is dependent. Always in the novel's background is Douce, whose quality of detachment represents a genuine freedom: undemanding in her simplicity, she never requires the sustenance of love—as opposed to pure sensuality—and she exists only to give pleasure. She is useless except as a love-object; hers is the only perfection capable of attracting Alban.[7] There is tragedy implied in Douce's uselessness beyond the realm of physical pleasure, for sentimental love lies beyond Alban's emotional scale; indeed, Montherlant's works consistently portray sentimentality as a human weakness.

Alban leaves for the trenches because Prinet is already at the front and not because France needs another soldier. Their comradeship depends primarily upon *dominio,* for Alban must dominate his friend if only because he finds him unworthy. Prinet cannot shake off the specter of Paris, of his bourgeois milieu with all of its false standards. In one sadistic episode, Alban insists that Prinet's dog be killed—and Alban does finally kill his friend's mascot. As usual, the sadistic movement is followed immediately by remorse, a very twisted remorse, to be sure. Later, when Prinet is wounded and dies at the front, Alban tries relentlessly to find him and to make amends for the work of his *dominio;* as soon as Alban learns of the death, he sinks into a deep depression. While the novel does underline Alban's rejection of need and his ecstasy in liberty, it really exposes his real need for others.[8] For Alban everything meaningful in life springs from contact with others. Hence, by a strange arrangement of logic, Prinet's death is a symbolic death of war itself and of all that it signifies: personal freedom is in jeopardy and patriotism is a nullity. The war, after all, is an unreal stage, a senseless dream.[9] Finally, Alban rejects war as a portion of his liberty.[10]

Le Songe is also a novel treating Alban's rejection and renunciation of Dominique. Originally cast as a symbol of perfection both physical and intellectual, she condemns herself almost at the beginning of the story by expressing to Alban her need for him. In Montherlantian psychology the weakness of dependence leads inevitably to final renunciation and indifference. Dominique's intelligence is dominated by her sensitivity, by her emotions, and by her genuine love for Alban: she is therefore doomed. Diminished in Alban's eyes precisely because she does love him in the sentimental sense—her love is always contrasted with Douce's—she is even further condemned because she follows him to the front. Dominique, as nurse and as girl in love, scarcely draws attention; we are always drawn to Alban's calculated sadism. His physical desire for Dominique is aroused only when she is weakened by his constant mental torture. Whenever she is rational and normal, she is most distant from Alban's interest.[11]

Montherlant possesses imagination in his depiction of humans diminished by cruelty. In a scene designed to add a quality of the absurd to a portrayal of sadism, Alban chews gum—an act signifying his indifference—all the while Dominique pleads with him for love. The curious destruction of love as Montherlant describes it is repeated at a later point of the novel when Dominique arranges to meet Alban in a hotel room. There, out of her social and moral element, Dominique experiences the chaos of a woman drawn relentlessly to one more defeat. Dominique, like Prinet and like the war, is an instrument used by Alban to find an identity that has no meaning.

Alban can neither find himself nor explain his strange behavior. But he does understand the bestial within himself that defies the rational. His character is later developed as Costals in *Les Jeunes Filles;* indeed, Alban is the prototype of the Montherlantian hero, for whom sensual love is a transient portion of life's chaos—and sentimental love chaos itself.[12] Alban's dependence on others erases his own power, and *dominio* is false. We are not concerned with an unreal monster in Alban de Bricoule, however. Psychologists recognize the sufferings of the strong when they are at the mercy of the weak. Alban belongs to Montherlant's mystique of Rome for, like all of his heroes, he eventually meets defeat. His aloneness is a form of self-imposed destruction that ends in oblivion.

I think that *Le Songe* is not a very good novel, primarily because the author places Alban in a war whose scenes draw one's attention away from the real focus: Alban's search for identity. But it is an important work because of its definition of the universal man.

III Les Olympiques

The conceptual framework of *Les Olympiques* (1924) is so vague, its definitions so disparate, that critics hesitate to pigeonhole too hastily a work perhaps meant to be different and original. It was written between 1920 and 1924, in time to be published when the Olympic Games were held in Paris in 1924. The several parts that comprise *Les Olympiques*—prose, poetry, and drama—are novelistic only insofar as they are held together by the young protagonist Jacques Peyrony; their unity is the subject of sports. The work is devoted to sports, of course, and to the furthering of health, vigor, and character building. Montherlant's contribution is to add intelligence to the commonly accepted values; for him sports without intelligence have no meaning. But he does not stop with intelligence: he adds a final quality, poetry. Montherlant does not sidestep the mystique of Rome, of course, for *dominio,* now with intelligence and poetry, is the sense of competition.

Again, he glorifies sports as a means of attaining order in a chaotic world. He maintains that understanding and friendship are born and nurtured in the stadium, and that they are lost beyond the stadium's gates. This attitude does not represent a new view, for the Albans and the Costals are also born and nurtured in a sort of "stadium," and it prepares them for battle with worldly chaos. Montherlant finds among athletes the basic primitivism, the sensuality, and the sense of being *engagé,* all of which could make more sound a society he deems mediocre. Order in society would then lead to national order and harmony. Here, unfortunately, Montherlant becomes a sociologist whose ideas we cannot take too seriously. His clearest statement of *Les Olympiques* concerns the power of sports to push human emotions to a second rank of importance: that is where they should be in the mystique.[13]

I have noted that Jacques Peyrony is the hero of *Les Olym-*

piques. In point of fact, sport itself is the hero and Jacques Peyrony is its spokesman. There are antagonists in the work, as well: Peyrony's parents are traced with bitter hatred—although more by the writer than by the boy. As parents they summarize the idiocies of bourgeois mores, of pusillanimity; they cannot understand the intellectual-poetic view of sports and certainly not the author's own élan. In this strange lyric work they represent a cancerous-like disorder eating away at grandeur (sports), and they threaten society itself.

Les Olympiques will attract a few sensitive youths in their own lyric years and in love with sports. The subject is not precisely suited to a lyric theme, for it is rather difficult to become emotionally involved with a poetic selection titled "To a Girl Victorious in the 1,000 Meter Race." It would be a mistake, however, to pass over certain values offered by the work. First, Montherlant defines chaos as a description of the world, and it is a term he will continue to use. Second, he again describes isolation—the athlete's—and a defiance of society. Finally, his competition in sports will change into the hero's constant struggle against his peers and inferiors. Exposure to the mob beyond the stadium blemishes and taints the pure soul of the athlete-hero, and Montherlant, I think, regrets that life is not a stadium.

IV Les Bestiaires (The Matador)

With *Les Bestiaires* (1926) Montherlant returns more clearly to the mystique of Rome; modern athletism is forgotten. Now the athlete is transformed into a gladiator—whence comes the title—who faces a worthy opponent in the form of a bull. It is Montherlant's best lyric work, surely, because its theme is more genuinely convincing: Montherlant was interested in bullfighting at the age of nine and had fought his first bulls in 1911. The hero of the novel is again Alban de Bricoule, and *Les Bestiaires* together with *Le Songe* are grouped by the author under the general title *La Jeunesse d'Alban de Bricoule.* Such a grouping is somewhat arbitrary, however, since the two novels do not form a comprehensive whole and the second novel is not the sequel of the first.

The author transfers to his readers the emotional tension of *Les Bestiaires.* Alban at the outset of the novel is almost possessed: he is frantically anxious to leave Paris for Spain where he can be free (from caste) in a world of grandeur. As he crosses the border into Spain he feels an immense surge of relief as he mentally discards the mediocrities of his bourgeois world. During his first days his sole dedication is to seek out information concerning corridas that might interest him; he carries out his task with the passion of love.[14] Alban's passion is more than a simple love affair with a national tradition, for an intellectual concern with a cult is at the root of his devotion. The novel's incantatory passages addressed to Mithra, as well as a thorough documentation of bullfighting in Spain and in Rome, clear the way for an understanding of the work as a formal devotion to a mystique. But Alban in singing of Mithra does not abandon the Christian: his songs are a careful mingling of the Christian and the Mithraic, with the result that the one is harmonious with the other.

Montherlant leaves nothing to the reader's imagination in his novel of the corrida; his work lifts his reader to a new level of understanding of bullfighting. Even those who find bullfighting no sport at all can understand the sense of the cult as well as Montherlant's intense focus upon the cult's priest, Alban. If one is not persuaded to like bullfighting, one is nevertheless awed by the intensity and thoroughness with which Montherlant attempts to write a lyric history of the tradition. It is also difficult not to savor Alban's dream-like progression from ecstasy to his final encounter with his bull, which he calls "le mauvais ange." I find the novel's "Epilogue" of particular interest since it, too, resembles an incantation and extends the mystique to Mediterranean France. Of course, Montherlant's intention in *Les Bestiaires* is to justify human participation in a peculiar mystery of life—as he understands it—and he achieves a remarkable success in explaining it to the uninitiated.

The novel is Montherlant's clearest example of a Christian-pagan dualism, although I remain unconvinced of the author's wish to emphasize the Christian aspects of the novel or a Christian morality in Alban de Bricoule. There is too much evidence that Alban's Christianity (or Catholicism) is, like Montherlant's, sentimentally heraldic, a portion of his caste he does not wish to renounce. Dogma is not really a concern of the novel, for only parallels of reference seem striking: Alban wishes to mold Catholicism to fit militant Mithraism. One has only to note the references to bullfighting in Papal Rome. Certainly, there is no hint that Alban (Montherlant) strives to transform Mithraism into Catholicism. In one segment of the novel, as Alban visits the arena on the eve of his combat with the bull, he senses a reconciliation of the two religions: the Church always seems to look down on the arena as a sustaining force, with Mithra and Christ in union.[15] For some, Alban's attempt to create such a reconciliation may seem preposterously barbaric or blasphemous, especially when he occasionally refers to the Mass.[16] We are concerned, however, less with blasphemy than with lyricism. He is entirely lyric, for example, when he becomes intrigued with a symbolism of blood, and he associates the blood of the (Christian) lamb with that of the bull. In the slaughterhouse, where the dead bulls are carved up after the drama of the bullring, Alban notes the relationship between the Christian church and the abattoir, both ringing with "benedictions," symbolizing the Christian-pagan divinity.[17] The cult of blood as part of a divine sacrifice is found again in the "Epilogue" to *Les Bestiaires,* although this time cast in the poetry and language of the French Camargue.[18]

Such reflections of a wish for religious union are sprinkled throughout the work. Montherlant's intention is to describe a cult of heroic proportions, and he accomplishes his task with painstaking care, although always subjectively. Remarkably, the final scene of the novel does not depict the glory of the matador in a noble posture near the dying bull, nor does it depict the matador's pride in the accomplishment of a ritual. Because it is a cult, understood always to be entirely serious, completely religious and unsentimental, it diminishes everything "worldly." The audience at the bullring, for example, has little importance in the novel, since the spectators signify mass mediocrity and they should never be permitted to participate in the cult's sacredness. Somewhere near the beginning of the novel Montherlant might have preferred to proclaim his own "Ite, missa est" to disperse the crowd and to let Alban serve at his bloody altar of sacrifice in solitude.

If Alban is the priest, he has his acolyte. The novel's final moments in the abattoir focus momentarily upon the boy Jesús, who has the job of helping to carve up the recently killed bull. His name—common enough in Spain—is aptly chosen by Montherlant, who carefully pursues all of the possibilities of his symbolism. Jesús is an urchin paid to do a miserable task. Yet Alban is drawn to the boy, especially to the symbolic rôle he plays in the Mithraic-Christian drama; Alban is grateful that he is able to share with his acolyte the sacrifice of blood.[19]

While the novel's principal interest and importance is in its portrayal of the cult—a portion of Montherlant's mystique as envisioned and lived passionately by Alban—it also has secondary themes. But there is a confusion here, much as there is a confusion in sorting out the elements of *Le Songe:* in *Les Bestiaires* the incantatory passages, the songs of the cult, often appear as obfuscations of the plot. The reader is forced to encounter other characters, such as Soledad and her family. Yet Soledad, and especially her world, serves to muddy the direction of the novel; Montherlant must have created her and others in order to adhere to novelistic form and plot structure. As the daughter of Alban's host, Soledad emerges as a typical Montherlantian "heroine," for she suggests Andrée Hacquebaut of *Les Jeunes Filles* or even Dominique of *Le Songe.* She is an instrument of Alban's cult, since she has a usefulness—an *utilité*—for him, but she appears and disappears from the novel like a figure moving in and out of a Swiss thermometer. Her usefulness is a negative one: she represents a sort of human deformation existing to deform others and to weaken and deplete the male *dominio.* Alban performs for her and is furious because she has the power to make him perform. He comments acidly on the duties of knights in the Middle Ages, whose acts, never noble in Alban's view, were so often inspired ignominiously by their ladies; indeed, feudal gallantry is thoroughly undermined in *Les Bestiaires.* Soledad, however, as she is described by Montherlant, is really a shadow of a woman. Clearly, the relationship between Alban and Soledad cannot support a plot devoted to the cult. Sensuality is left for the arena, for the contest between man and beast, and Soledad's sensuality is undermined and constantly diminished. In one scene, a scene I believe not meant to be humorous, Alban is forced to sit behind Soledad's enormously elaborate coiffure springing from a powdered neck. He is angry with her because she is in his line of vision, but he is primarily annoyed because she stands as a symbol of the crowd unworthy of participating in the cult. Later, as Alban's religiosity mounts in anticipation of his day in the ring, the memory of Soledad weakens and finally disappears completely.

Similarly, the novel is weakened by Montherlant's superficial treatment of minor characters who are imposed upon the plot. Foreigners in Madrid ruin Alban's path to his cult—and to his identity. He is scarcely able to endure the sight of Frenchmen unless they are from "Mediterranean" France, the Camargue, for example. He protests against the presence of the insidious American, the fatuous Englishman, and so on: these outsiders are the destroyers of the cult's grandeur and sanctity.

Montherlant, of course, transfers to Alban the concept of *casta* as replacement for French caste, which he holds in less esteem. Yet Montherlant's caste shows through: Alban thinks in terms of "perfidious" Albion; the American Yankee is a diminished soul seen partly through French eyes and partly as the enemy of Spain's grandeur. In creating such bizarre departures from the plot, Montherlant demonstrates his inability, at least in *Les Bestiaires,* to avoid casual social commentary of little consequence to the work itself.

Hence, *Les Bestiaires* is not a well-constructed novel. In spite of its faults, it still rivals Hemingway's *Death in the Afternoon* as a prose poem devoted to a cult. The work possesses the youthful lyric quality of the early Montherlant not yet given to acrimony. Readers will be fascinated, I think, with the artistry of Montherlant's poetry and with the strange definitions of the bullring. As hero, Alban of *Les Bestiaires* is less the prototype of Montherlant's later characters: Alban is fulfilled in this novel, but the Alban of *Le Songe* is defeated. Yet both Albans represent facets of the Montherlantian universal man.

V La Petite Infante de Castille

Like *Les Olympiques* difficult to classify by genre, *La Petite Infante de Castille* (1929) consists of a thin plot woven with the threads of the *culte du moi;* it defies definition. The "historiette"—for want of a better term—is partly diary and partly expository, but it does have that very thin thread one may wish to call plot. It derives from Montherlant's mature personal crisis of post-adolescence during the period of his wanderings in the Mediterranean worlds of Europe and Africa. What we see in this curiously wrought work is the edge of crisis, never the core. In a real sense, it should be read together with the essays of *Aux fontaines du désir* (1927) and of *Un Voyageur solitaire est un diable* (1945), devoted to the same period of personal crisis, in order to grasp the sense of Montherlant's own chaos. At the risk of proposing a weak hypothesis, I believe that Montherlant may have attempted, in Part I of *La Petite Infante de Castille,* to sketch the beginnings of a novel.

It is clear that the lyricism of 1929 emerges from an emotional and intellectual turmoil of some consequence. In one sense *La Petite Infante de Castille* is a sequel to *Les Bestiaires,* if only because the subject is Spain. In the former work Barcelona replaces Seville, however, and sensualism rather than the cult of the bullring dominates. Part I, containing the essence of Montherlant's diary, has as its theme the traditional Spanish tale of a knight who encounters the Castillian Infanta in a tree; because he consults his mother about what to do next, he loses her to another.[20] Obviously, Montherlant proposes the tale to underline the necessity for action at all cost. But a major plot that might emanate from the legend is left to die, for instead of pursuing the story's implication in some imaginative way, he pauses to philosophize on the nature of women, especially of Spanish women. His remarks are entirely favorable, of course, for he sees Spanish women as beauties of the nineteenth century; they have not acquired the artificiality of the present century—as have Frenchwomen, for example. His digressions recall those met throughout *Les Jeunes Filles,* for these later novels also show the Montherlantian penchant for asides. It is nevertheless true that Montherlant really wishes to discuss personal liberty, one that can be found only in the Mediterranean worlds. *La Petite Infante de Castille* is essentially an expression of the author's own liberation from caste, from the bleak north, and from the materialism of his Parisian milieu. By the same token the war of *Le Songe* is meant to be a release from bonds; the cult of bullfighting is also a liberation of self. Now, in *La Petite Infante de Castille,* all of Spain symbolizes freedom: only there is syncretic man given scope. Montherlant would like to be a Spaniard, of course, and there is a distinct parallel between Alban's World War I—a world he cannot know—and Montherlant's Spain. He can never be a Spaniard and he knows it. Forever the alien in a seemingly ideal world, his Spanishness is a mask that sometimes becomes intolerable; it also tends to pervert his reasoning.

Outside of the legendary context and at the level of plot the Infanta is a music hall dancer, Dolores López, whom the "I" of the novel—Montherlant—wishes to meet. Curiously, Dolores López as a novelistic character never emerges from the pages of the book except for a brief moment. With the help of an aging matador, Puig, the "I" does finally meet the girl, but the encounter is studied, calculated, and overly intellectualized. Furthermore, nothing happens: the "hero" suddenly renounces Dolores and rushes back to France. There is in this renunciation—a familiar

Montherlantian theme—the smell of death, a swerving from life. France becomes in the end a refuge from the sensual Spain, and there, in what is to Montherlant the climate of unbearable but familiar mediocrity, are to be found the comforting qualities of a familiar existence: France is the haven for the prodigal son.

Defeat lies well within the reach of Montherlant's syncretic man. Renunciation and flight, the two principal concepts of Part I, are unfolded and revealed with a bitter tone. Knowledge of one's perpetual alienation from an ideal, of one's inability to melt somehow into a beloved culture, leads to desperation. It also explains Montherlant's battle of love and hate with Spain.[21] Montherlant also underlines the importance of self-domination, of the will to turn away abruptly from the sensual world by means of *dominio* over the self. In Part II of *La Petite Infante de Castille,* the rejection of Dolores has no force and is no longer an issue, and thinking about her is an annoyance. Somewhat like Rimbaud intellectually and spiritually exhausted by too much erotic-poetic involvement, Montherlant turns his back on what he considers to be a false idealism. His "Ile de la Félicité"—the title of a poem devoted to the sensual in Part II—treats the exquisite perfection of such an idealism, an idealism now to be avoided. On his "island" he wants a greater joy, but it is not accompanied by happiness. Of course, Montherlant will demonstrate in *Les Jeunes Filles* that happiness is an impossible state and is never achieved.

As for the Spain of *La Petite Infante de Castille,* it is examined in curious fashion and never with the same eyes that view the Spain of *Les Bestiaires.* The opening paragraphs describe a train jammed with passengers bound together in common chaos and in a world of inefficiency. Here, in the later work, Montherlant observes the reverse of the coin: Spain possesses a mediocrity because it is sinking under the weight of filth and progress and is apparently trying to emulate the worst elements of northern Europe's progress. Why does Montherlant suddenly revolt against a vast portion of his mystique? It is his natural instinct to lash out at the beloved object capable of deceiving and of betraying. The glorious Seville of *Les Bestiaires* is replaced by a Madrid stifled by its monarchy, by a Toledo representing both beauty and boredom, by a Grenada seen as an enormous deception, and by a Saragossa unworthy of esteem. He does still acknowledge, although reluctantly, the grandeur of Seville; indeed, Spain for Montherlant means Seville.

La Petite Infante de Castille should be studied primarily for its themes: renunciation-rejection-death, and flight as a symbolic death. It is an important means to grasp a new understanding of the sensual related to man's *dominio* and to observe the multiplicity of facets that comprise universal man. It is a transition work, the negation of *Les Bestiaires,* and it serves as an excellent introduction to *Les Jeunes Filles.*

CHAPTER 3

The Solitary Hero: Novels of Chaos and Darkness

I *Montherlant's "roman-roman," or, the Objective Novel*

WITH *Les Célibataires* (1934) Montherlant clearly abandons the lyricism of his early period and devotes himself to what he terms the objective novel, or the "roman-roman." Some critics, among them Roger Secrétain, hold to the thesis that the unpublished *La Rose de sable* should be counted as the first of the objective novels. Concerning this non-existent work, about which there is so much speculation, Montherlant simply explains that its publication might tend to be awkward because it is supposedly an exposé of French colonial policy in North Africa. In final analysis, there is little point in trying to ferret out the quality of *La Rose de sable*, as Jean de Beer has done, and we must accept Montherlant's final word on the matter.[1]

What should really concern us is the term objectivity. Its use to describe the later novels implies correctly that the prose works of the lyric period emanate from Montherlant's diaries. The author insists, however, that with *Les Célibataires* he removes himself from his novels and that they must be understood as entities apart from him. Of course, many portions of works of the lyric period are augmentations and transformations of the author and cannot always be treated as simple reflections of his private life. In the objective works he establishes a continuum of thought first glimpsed in *Le Songe*, but he develops it and gives it depth. He creates new heroes—as well as non-heroes—of grander scope, and he becomes increasingly more capable of disciplining his creation in such a manner that he achieves characterizations in depth: his characterizations are more generally understood as studies of the human condition. They cease to be only minuscule depictions of man at odds with the self. In retrospect, the two Albans—I prefer to insist on the separateness of the two heroes—are in the throes of romantic poetry: Alban of *Le Songe* moves within the smallest of worlds from which he never escapes. Alban of *Les Bestiaires* sings the praises of the liberating cult of bullfighting, but his own world is an intellectualized one doomed to defeat—it is a defeat expressed, however, in *La Petite Infante de Castille,* which serves as the novel's postlude. But the bachelors of *Les Célibataires,* Costals of *Les Jeunes Filles,* and Celestino of *Le Chaos et la nuit*—the novels of the second period—represent facets of a single, but new, protagonist in heroic crisis. The characters are complicated examples of the universal man described in "Syncrétisme et alternance." Montherlant's multifaceted human animal is permitted to grow and to proceed to the several fates that await him. There is really no conclusion visible in the first novels; in the later novels the author does furnish conclusions, always unhappy ones. Neither Léon de Coantré, nor Costals, nor Celestino is a Montherlant or a Montherlantian mask, although they are aspects of his universal man.

It is clear that there is an unfortunate consequence of an argument that insists upon the autobiographical nature of the objective works. Elie de Coëtquidan, Léon de Coantré, and Octave, the three bachelors of *Les Célibataires,* are not men to emulate, for they are negatively drawn as the wretched hulks of a sterile and worn nobility. By the same token, the artist-writer Costals of *Les Jeunes Filles* is a monster of willful and conscious cruelty, depicted as having no redeeming qualities. His creativity, which might tend in part to excuse his weaknesses in a curious world of inadequate or senseless women, is scarcely touched upon. Again, Celestino of *Le Chaos et la nuit* is a wreck of a man whose life is devoted to senseless self-destruction. Montherlant treats all of these characters without indulgence or sympathy to such a remarkable degree that the reader's few brief waves of understanding are in inevitable conflict with the grotesqueness and horror they display. Montherlant emphasizes their implacable nihilism.[2] But I sense nowhere in Montherlant's own experience a descent into the complete nihilism of his characters: his creativity is sufficient to lift him from such depths. Of course, absolute objectivity on the part of any author is hard to come by.

His creative process in the later novels is worthy of note. One can never be sure whether Montherlant is more at ease in writing a novel or in writing a play. We know that he attempted drama at an early age: the two genres run a parallel path throughout his life. Certainly, the technique of drama emerges from the pages of *Les Célibataires,* which may be called a tragic drama in the form of the novel. As tragedy it offers a clear exposition, a plot development with divisions, or acts, that move with force and energy toward a dénouement whose inevitability is understood from the first page. Again, *Le Chaos et la nuit* lends itself to a similar dramatic analysis. On the other hand, the four novels of *Les Jeunes Filles* unfold their movement in an entirely different way: the author chooses to follow bizarre paths that defy normal analysis. The principal path has the flavor of the epistolary novel: there are even selections from a magazine devoted to the lovelorn. Montherlant's penchant for dramatic form is then best seen in *Les Célibataires* and *Le Chaos et la nuit,* where there is a disciplined attempt to limit time and space into acts and scenes.

With respect to the continuum of themes, Montherlant offers in the later novels what is merely suggested or imperfectly depicted in the lyric works. Now renunciation, destruction, especially self-destruction, and the inevitable *dominio* blend to become an unshaded despair in a world that Montherlant calls chaos. For that reason, I have called his major novelistic efforts the "novels of chaos and darkness"; in doing so, I draw upon the title of his latest novel, which so clearly portrays that despair. On the surface, the novels seem widely divergent, but their themes can be reduced to man's condition in various atmospheres: the nobility, the world of women, the world of anarchy.

II Les Célibataires (The Bachelors)

Les Célibataires (1934) is about men defeated at birth because of their birth. The grandeur of nobility in this novel is expressed negatively: a baron's crown impressed lavishly on a faded calling card, a careful formal use of *vous,* a flashback to a former generation of unsettling dignity. What is impressive is the aura of grandeur, fading and meaningless, that the reader must imagine: it is an aura of unchanging intensity covering the immediate reality of personal ruin. Montherlant spares no one in this novel of decadent Breton nobility. Dignity is expressed only in the character of the old housekeeper Mélanie, who punctuates the tragedy.

Baron Elie de Coëtquidan, sixty-four years old, shares the house on the Boulevard Arago in Paris with his nephew Count Léon de Coantré, fifty-three years old. The house, left to Léon by his mother (and Elie's sister), the Countess of Coantré, dead only six months before the novel begins, must be sold to settle the estate. But this news of financial dissolution sets the tragedy into motion;

it is only the last step of a long disintegration, and the loss of the house is only the final symbol of an end. If Elie is able to make a small monthly payment to Léon for his maintenance and to help with household affairs, Léon, on the other hand, has no fixed income: his mother's estate, devastated by seemingly countless claims against it, begins to dwindle into obscurity. And in February of 1924, the time of the novel's first action, Léon, always displaying a deference toward his uncle Elie, explains their need to move away from the house by October 15. Reason, of course, would suggest a way out of the family dilemma, for Elie at his age could exist in a boarding home, and Léon could still find employment to see him through a bleak period. But we are not concerned so much with reason as with caste and birth. There is no way out of the dilemma, for nobility is a curious wall that stands in the way of rational solution. Both men are utterly helpless.

Formerly, Léon had decided to join a friend, Levier, in a commercial enterprise. Such an undertaking would certainly have been enhanced by having a title of the nobility attached to it. It failed, however, and at that point of failure Léon resigned from life.[3] There had been a question of marriage, but it was quickly forgotten when it became clear that Léon, treated by his mother always as a toy, would have his way in turning aside all responsibilities. He seconded his commercial bankruptcy by a bankruptcy of life itself.[4] At his age Léon's attempts to find work would be empty gestures. Unaware of reality, he is not filled with despair at the idea of moving from his house; instead, the details of moving give him a sense of pleasure, and the move itself elates him.

Léon's apparent madness finds its counterpart in Elie. Elie had forty years in which to learn how to stop living. Like Léon, he seems unable and unwilling to cope with his life or with life around him, and he resembles something af a latter-day *honnête homme*—the gentleman of the seventeenth century—thrown headlong into an ungentlemanly era.[5] Montherlant also traces the basic evil of Elie, equal to that of Elie's father: the author underlines the fact that his tragedy probably stems from two defects: he dresses poorly and is inadequate sexually.

Such forms of madness in Léon and Elie are persuasive indeed: they appear at several levels to consternate the reader. Conversations at mealtimes become insidiously inane, and communication has no meaning. Yet from time to time reason does find its way into the insanity of their conversations, and what seems to be madness is truth.[6] It would be a mistake to think that celibacy itself is at the root of the madness Montherlant traces. He does not very often touch on the problem of celibacy, but rather moves to what is celibacy's offspring: anxiety. He also notes that bitterness inevitably accompanies aging.[7] Although endowed with noble blood, Léon's blood is watered down and barely able to sustain life. His nobility is a state of mind: a noble *is* and does not *do*. Hence, he is forever on the brink of oblivion. Léon displays more clearly than Elie this madness that is really a total unawareness of life. One can sympathize with him, perhaps, much as one sympathizes with a victim of mental illness. Léon appears as a child man who has spent twenty years in undoing every portion of his human value. With a remaining shadow of reason he tries to help Elie, who senses the meaning of his defeat and vaguely acknowledges the painful existence to come. But his last shadow of reason also has its touch of madness: he offers Elie a hearty *sursum corda!* as empty of meaning as his life.

Léon's anxiety randomly shows through his moments of strange optimism. It develops whenever he must face relatively minor problems—the major problems do not bother him. Montherlant claims that the tragedy of anxious people stems from the fact that their anxiety is justified.[8] When Léon is confronted with the problems of the estate, for example, or with Mélanie's departure, he feels a euphoria, which one may ascribe to martyrdom. Her leaving has a fatalistic nature as part of an inevitable doom, but he is able to accept it because he cannot control it. Léon moves continuously between euphoria and anxiety as the novel progresses; his anxiety will finally dominate.

As anxiety more clearly replaces his euphoria, it leads Léon closer to self-destruction; actual suicide, however, never invades the development of the novel. Instead, Léon's long life of self-destroying activity is followed by an unconscious wish for death. It is also an escapism expressed through sleep, a refuge to which Léon turns with greater frequency as his life pushes toward the October crisis.[9] Indeed, to insure sleep he asks Mélanie to prepare heavier meals. Finally, he never awakens to reality in any form.

Alone after his move from the house to Fréville, Léon exists—or rather, he vegetates—in a housekeeper's cottage made available to him by his uncle Octave. There, in an atmosphere of total isolation, he continues to "die" in still greater stretches of escape from time. When actual death comes, it is little more than a different sort of sleep. Much as a dying man may somehow catch a glimpse of a meaning of life, Léon before his death at last grasps the sense of his futile years: he realizes that his life has depended exclusively on a show of pride that has always removed him from the obligation of coping with reality.[10] Renunciation and rejection of all things, but always in the name of pride, become the stuff of human dignity for Léon.

III *Evaluation of* Les Célibataires

The title of Montherlant's novel is somewhat ambiguous, for its plurality suggests that the novel treats at least Elie and Léon as the bachelors; but Octave is also included. Montherlant presents another problem by seeming to stress, at the beginning of *Les Célibataires,* Elie de Coëtquidan as his foremost character. Indeed the work's opening passages strongly suggest a Balzacian influence: objects and persons are seen first in the general focus and finally in a detailed view. Attention is always drawn toward Elie, however, for what he wears and what he carries serve to announce his character. What is surprising is Montherlant's intention to let the character of Léon dominate the work, at least after the beginning pages: he is justified in turning to Léon, however, because his tragedy is clearer than Elie's. Octave as the third bachelor is a less persuasive character. He is a successful banker, albeit spiritually unsound and absurd, and is totally wrapped up in his selfish interests; his great defect is his unwillingness to use his money or his influence for the salvation of his own kind.

If Octave is the third bachelor of the novel, although seemingly serving no novelistic need, he is traced in an amusing way. An Americanophile, he supposedly reflects the American businessman's views of the world—and even has a rocking chair. He is also an Anglophile and claims that the London *Daily Mail,* which he cannot read intelligently, helps him get at the heart of French politics. In fact a latter-day "bourgeois gentilhomme," he is a social climber using his title as a lever to open new doors. He would be merely laughable were he not caught up in Léon's tragedy; selfish, he sacrifices Léon because he is an uninteresting object standing in the way of his own grandeur. Somehow, Montherlant leaves Octave in limbo just as he leaves Elie in an inconclusive state. And yet I find here one of Montherlant's excellent talents: his ability to paint faithfully and accurately the emptiness of man paralyzed by some unusual force that may not even appear as a major one. Seen in this light, Léon, Elie, and Octave are all worthy of close scrutiny.

Two segments of *Les Célibataires* will undoubtedly endure as masterpieces of psychological analysis. The first segment concerns the adventure of Léon in Montmartre; it is a study of a man's defeat in the midst of sensual pleasures. In a café Léon tries desperately to look busy by writing and ineffectually seeks to attract the attention of a woman seated nearby. At the same time a local prostitute repeatedly tries to approach him, to tease him, and certainly to distract him from his writing. But his writing is entirely mindless, for it consists of copying items from the bill submitted by the funeral home for his mother's funeral. Montherlant's mature style is again evident in the final scenes of the novel. His description of Léon's death and of the aftermath demonstrates a disciplined brevity. No longer able to speak for himself because he is dead, Léon's testament is left in his unpaid bills; and because of an item for alcohol, he is assumed to have died of alcoholism. Montherlant has avoided pathos in underlining the scope of total absurdity.[11]

I have already pointed out what I consider to be the weakness of *Les Célibataires*: Montherlant's curious change of direction away from Elie and toward Léon, as well as his somewhat feeble portrayal of Octave. Yet there are few faults to find with this first major novel. It is a superb commentary on a fading caste—the Breton nobility—although caste in the general sense seems of greater concern than nobility in the specific sense. It is more accurate to call the novel a study of suicide, a suicide made inevitable because Léon never lives on a par with people but rather on a par with pride. If he is a non-person, he is also a non-hero, for he never meets fate, struggles with obstacles, or tries to prevail. Lacking in intelligence, he cannot understand his defeat. Montherlant captures every shading of this curious creature, often in excessively long descriptive passages, but again in well-disciplined pages among the best of our century.[12]

IV *The Tetralogy* Les Jeunes Filles

1. LES JEUNES FILLES (YOUNG GIRLS). In his foreword to the novels of the tetralogy Montherlant writes that he sees Costals as disquieting and odious. This description seems mild indeed, for Costals emerges in the first novel *Les Jeunes Filles* (1936) as a monster of cynicism and selfishness. In effect, he is a non-hero

in the throes of a personal chaos, although he does not understand its precise nature; it is a chaos that demands its victims. They are the unusually neurotic women whose contacts with Costals are the focus of the four novels. Despite the title of the tetralogy, whose apparent emphasis is directed toward the women, and despite Montherlant's elaborate treatment of them as studies in feminine psychology, Costals alone gives definition to the works. If Costals is a non-hero, the novels are essays on the subject of non-love, for Costals' nihilism undermines the sense of love. Costals appears to be in a constant struggle to realize some sort of rational life as a primitive for whom love means only a sensual relationship totally devoid of sentimentality. Costals accepts the necessity of human relationships, but they must be shorn of adornments he deems debilitating or time-consuming, and they cannot impose responsibilities. To be sure, he does not deny affection and tenderness providing they refrain from imposing their power to seduce man's freedom. Hence, the concept of "falling in love" or of "being in love" makes no sense; similarly, marriage imposes itself as an enormous bondage to be avoided at all cost. Women in love, according to Costals, are little more than useless burdens, and their devotion to marriage—or perhaps to imagined ideals symbolized in the marriage ceremonial—is their greatest weakness. Such views, however, are not those of Costals the primitive but rather of Costals the artist. The novels then portray a man who thinks he is primitive but who is always intellectualized and intellectualizing.

Costals' nihilism, established early in the tetralogy, marks a private hell of which he is unaware. Worse, he uses love as a psychological laboratory of experimentation and hopes his experiments will provide him matter for his literary creation. Naturally, the writer Costals, whose *dominio* over his women is always understood to prevail, will serve as constant hero for such works. But Costals never seems aware that he is deformed, that he moves constantly against life, that his victims push him toward his own defeat. Instead of being a creative artist totally devoted to the creative process, he proceeds toward a form of death. Costals consciously or unconsciously rejects life much as he rejects women. In ridding himself of human obstacles—women in love, for example—he appears as a man who merely exists on the fringe of life, although he believes he exists only to create. To create what? The question is never answered. Yet the reader feels sympathy for Costals from time to time, despite his evil.

His monstrosity is not entirely of his own invention, for the women of *Les Jeunes Filles* throw themselves at him, or else they demonstrate a martyr complex as astonishing as Costals' willingness to help create their martyrdom. The women seek him out—he does not seek them—by writing fan letters of revolting sentimentality. The letters reflect their wish for some sort of impossible freedom they cannot define. All, save for Solange Dandillot, are intellectually weak, emotionally unsound, and irrevocably provincial. Whether they discuss religion, friendship, family, or "great ideas," they demonstrate to what degree they depend on sustenance from others—preferably artists—capable of translating their visions into substantial meaning: they seek, perhaps without being aware of it, a glorification, even an elevation, in an association with an artist whose creativity is forever closed to them.

The best example of the pitiable condition of such neurotic women is expressed in the character of Thérèse Pantevin, whose letters to Costals are drenched in religiosity rather than in religion. Thérèse's soul is bleached of divine meaning, and Costals replaces Christ as the object of her devotions. If her letters seem outrageous manifestations of a very sick woman, Costals' replies are the equally outrageous demonstrations of a very lost mind. He writes first to tell her to forget him, for he cannot reciprocate her feelings; he suggests later that she go to a nunnery to serve her God with heart and soul—just as he serves literature.

Another correspondent, Andrée Hacquebaut, participates more directly in Costals' life. In their first exchange of letters Andrée's expressions of sentimentality are in balance with Costals' caution and defensiveness. Their letters are little more than automatic gestures after a brief time: Costals imposes restrictions on their correspondence and informs Andrée of them as bluntly as possible. He is annoyed because Andrée's sentimentality, which he rejects out of hand, imposes on him obligations he refuses to accept. To deflect her emotional interest in him, he sends her books of English literature and tells her to get hold of herself. But he writes again to explain that close friendships—or attachments in any form—bore him; that being loved more than one loves is one of the crosses he has to bear; that one should never reveal emotions to a loved one without asking forgiveness; and that love, after all, is only the invention of women. What is abundantly important to Costals is a circumscribed relationship composed of affection and desire that he prefers not to call love.[13] Costals denies the power of love and accepts in its place only a temporary gratification intended to satisfy his own needs: the movement of sensuality is always in one direction. In explaining the essence of his nature to Andrée Hacquebaut, he notes that pride, humility, dignity, plus an unceasing desire to remain free of human contact, direct him to his convictions of love's idiocy. Despite his "sensitivity," Costals continues to write to his "victims," especially to Andrée Hacquebaut, whose own dignity has long since disappeared in her provincial wilderness. Because of her sentimentality, she becomes the object of Costals' revulsion.

Andrée Hacquebaut, who lives in provincial Saint-Léonard, is a study of a woman doomed at the age of thirty to pursue meaningless values in a vacant world. Dying of boredom in the provinces, she dies a little faster when she comes to Paris to see Costals. Unfortunately she does not possess any quality of self-sufficiency or discipline that might permit her to meet new situations. Hers is a sentimentality that depends upon others; her sense of love has no depth and is fanned willy-nilly by the slightest masculine attention. In Paris to meet Costals, Andrée suffers an insidious martyrdom at his hands. She forever insists on a relationship which cannot possibly exist; Costals repeats with insistence that her affection for him is ridiculous. He supports his denunciation of her—and of all women who would stand in the way of art—by expounding on his hatred of marriage, of the uselessness of having children who become meaningless creatures. Indeed, Costals offers Andrée every opportunity to renounce the relationship. Somewhat reversing his determination to be rid of her, however, he does find her a job in Paris. But with unerring bad judgment Andrée devotes herself less to her job and more to interpreting literature; she becomes mindlessly concerned with Nietzsche, Valéry, and "pure poetry," and both she and her employer are relieved when she leaves the job. It is precisely her concern for life-through-literature that further reduces her value in Costals' eyes—in his world only men possess esthetic insights.

What is striking in the curiously drawn "relationship" between Costals and Andrée is their inability to communicate with each other. Andrée's emotions are as uncontrollable as Costals' intellectualized *dominio*. When reading *Les Jeunes Filles* I am constantly aware of listening to separate minds that never meet on the same subject; similarly, in their correspondence one letter never answers another. Of course, Costals' opinions always dominate, and Andrée's views, born of emotions, seem dim by contrast. She suggests a minor "confidante" in a drama, for she permits Costals to mouth his soliloquies, or *tirades,* devoted essentially to his quasi-heroic concern for grandeur and human intelligence, as well as to his mad poetry of absolute freedom. On this curious level of non-communication, however, Andrée proves interesting because she has the art of speaking truths within the framework of her mindless lack of logic. She is convincing, for example, when she tries to prove to Costals that he really loves her. Everything she says (and writes) seems rational, and every remark elicits further cruelty from Costals. He occasionally feels pangs of sympathy for her, but only whenever she is reduced by him to a pathetically small dimension.

Costals is not totally removed from human contact. His illegitimate son Philippe, whom he sees infrequently because he cannot endure the intimacy of the home, passes in and out of the novel like a pale ghost of the artist's past. Yet Philippe symbolizes Costals' nihilism in a curious way. Finding marriage impossible and children an unspeakable burden, Costals reflects that the only way to get along with a young boy is not to be his father. He likes his son but does not love him, and he likes him if the boy moves in a separate world: Philippe is cared for by Mademoiselle du Peyron de Larchant, a woman in her fifties who plays no rôle essential to the novel. During his visits to see Philippe, Costals plays unconvincingly at the game of fatherhood, but his legal hold on his son is no more justified than his forgotten sensual hold on the boy's mother, referred to cavalierly as the "chosen intermediary." Yet Philippe is perhaps the only meaningful creation that Costals has ever managed in his life.

Les Jeunes Filles proceeds from episode to episode with plodding pace. The epistolary form is followed by documentation, which in turn is followed by long passages of narration. Andrée Hacquebaut's visit to Paris is little more than a vignette, although in the novel's progression her visit is followed by further correspondence. Similarly, Costals' observations of the human animal and the human state serve to punctuate the work. What emerges from his thoughts—not altogether orderly—is a definition of human relationships that is too general. Montherlant sometimes forgets that he is supposed to be dealing with the artist's search for the ideal atmosphere for creativity.

Costals speaks too generally on the subject of happiness as a human condition, just as he speaks too omnisciently on the vast subjects of love and marriage. He proclaims that the search for happiness is not a male preoccupation, primarily because a man can never achieve it, but that women can have a positive idea of happiness although they never realize it. He adds that for women living is merely a matter of feeling. Hence, woman's fate leads her inevitably to marriage as a "natural" fulfillment and as a realization of her happiness. She is never entirely satisfied no matter what her condition in life becomes, and Costals concludes that a woman's lack of satisfaction is her normal condition. In lieu of happiness, a man can achieve only a state of peace. He notes that the majority of men marry without thinking just as they wage war without thinking, and he is assured that the world would die if men let pure reason guide them.[14] How far apart, then, are Costals and the Alban de Bricoule of *Le Songe?* Costals advocates sensual primitivism and rationalism for himself, and he accepts the irrational as the normal state of other men: he prefers that the others make a world capable of furnishing a peaceful existence for the artist-Costals. Unlike Alban, who recognizes his dependency on others, Costals rejects dependency in favor of isolation, or ivory-towerism. His is never a total isolation, for he needs others to feed his egotism, to feed his literature, and his needs create his inner chaos. A lack of communication lies at the heart of his chaotic existence—not so much on the level of language as on the level of emotions.

However grandiose may be his cynical outpourings supposedly couched in logic, they are of alternating patterns. His mind alternates according to his reactions of the moment. In a letter to his friend Pailhès, Costals admits to a feeling of sympathy, esteem, and admiration for Andrée—but only after she has left Paris. He sends an enlightening letter to Andrée, in which he describes his favorite types of women, none of which includes her. He also tells her that physical love is and would be a vast deception. He shifts thus between gentility and crudeness, between superficial tenderness and genuine brutality, and between inspiration and negation. All are facets of the same man, and all are equally true portions of Costals. We are dealing with a laboratory experiment in which

Montherlant creates a character, Costals, parading before our eyes the original sense of "Syncrétisme et alternance."

Since the four novels of *Les Jeunes Filles*—as title of the tetralogy—are portions of a serial, it is not surprising that Montherlant should introduce the most important feminine character toward the close of the first novel. Solange Dandillot is first mentioned in Costals' diary. A young woman in her twenties, she is attractive, Parisian, and perhaps not beside the point, she is the daughter of a man formerly devoted to sports. Costals is immediately attracted to her, although, true to his nature, he is fearful of the consequences of knowing her well; he also fears she may not like him. He is immensely relieved, for example, that an evening spent together at the Opéra-Comique does not make her fall in love with him and that his freedom is not in jeopardy. He treats Solange with surprising kindness at first because she does not belong to the band of women who seek out artists; besides, her aloofness is a challenge. He is nevertheless capable of cat-and-mouse tricks that bring him private amusement because they are daring. Bored with the concert, he makes playful love to Solange and then, without her knowledge and beyond her vision, he makes playful love to a woman seated next to Solange.[15] We should not assume that Costals is irrational, for his patterns of conduct follow Montherlantian definition: the syncretic Costals ceases to be believable only if we attempt to fit him into a "normal" view. His real reason for finally giving up his game with the strange woman is typical and utterly simple: he loses interest when he realizes that his arm is cramped. Typically, Solange's presence is forgotten in this ludicrous moment of the novel. We see only Costals' view of the theater: because he likes neither the music nor the audience, he notes that both are housed in a "temple of auto-suggestion."

Solange Dandillot, when she becomes Costals' mistress, is unlike Andrée, for her natural inclination is to be reserved. She cannot bring herself to use the informal *tu* with him.[16] She does not discuss at length the sense of love and continuously conjugate its implications. She also has a sense of good taste. Not a primitive soul, she does unconsciously make demands on Costals: he notes that he must arrange rendezvous, buy concert tickets, search for expensive restaurants. Unlike Andrée treated by Costals to drab rendezvous that mirror her drab provincial life, Solange never leaves her bourgeois milieu of banal comforts.

The first novel of the tetralogy has no dramatic conclusion whatsoever, and transitions are absent. We learn that Thérèse Pantevin experiences a deepening religious crisis—a madness linked with sexuality. Costals writes her a letter furthering her agony; he informs her that he will have compassion for her on a precise date at a precise hour. The last letter of the novel is a reply from Thérèse, who describes in minute detail a physiological-sexual-religious breakdown that happens at the time Costals has indicated. Thérèse's letters at the end of the novel, balancing with those of the novel's beginning, somehow create little unity: *Les Jeunes Filles* is an unfinished work without sense when read by itself. Of course, Montherlant uses Thérèse to serve as an example of the feminine mind incapable of intellectual powers, for she cannot cope with religion; there remains the implication that women in general cannot cope with it. Since Thérèse is mad, she does not offer a convincing case history. By the same token, of course, Andrée cannot cope with literature and philosophy. Nevertheless, the case histories of Thérèse and Andrée help to define the sense of Costals' hell on earth.

2. PITIÉ POUR LES FEMMES (PITY FOR WOMEN). Unlike the Balzacian novel, some of whose characters reappear in extensive portions of *La Comédie humaine,* Montherlant's tetralogy of *Les Jeunes Filles* offers an identical as well as an anticipated cast of characters. *Pitié pour les femmes* (1936), the second novel, presents no time gap and seems but a continuing series of chapters appended to the first novel. While each of Balzac's novels stands alone and possesses the unique quality of unity and totality—each novel having a complete sense by itself—the four parts of *Les Jeunes Filles* cannot effectively stand alone. Fully aware of his novels' interdependence, Montherlant has been obliged on occasion to annotate the second work with footnotes to guide the reader either unaware of the first work or else forgetful of its major lines of progression.

I have already mentioned the author's technique—although it might be called a defect—of placing Solange Dandillot at the end of the first novel and leaving her in limbo. The confusion is cleared up in *Pitié pour les femmes*, for Solange appears in it as a fully developed character. If Montherlant insists upon the necessity of the four works, he is perhaps wrong in assuming that readers may attempt to read all of them, and he may well have introduced Solange in the second of the novels in order to give it completeness. Andrée Hacquebaut, already shown as repressed like another Emma Bovary in the mediocrity of her provincial world, gains depth in *Pitié pour les femmes*. Montherlant seems to have taken more time to pin his strange creature to his examining board and to observe her more carefully with his magnifying glass. A further addition to the novel is a careful scrutiny of Solange's family; for the first time her parents become breathing humans rather than simple décor. What is abundantly evident in this work—as well as in the last two novels, *Le Démon du bien* and *Les Lépreuses*—is Montherlant's determination to accumulate good reasons for Costals' negative attitude toward women. The works then become case histories of masculine and feminine psychology, as Montherlant thinks he understand it, and they do little but continue the laboratory experiment begun in the first volume of the tetralogy.

The title of the second novel is in itself an example of the monstrous irony of which Montherlant is capable. Certainly, neither compassion nor pity are terms that describe Costals' treatment of Solange Dandillot, of Andrée Hacquebaut, or even of Thérèse Pantevin. Costals continues to subject Solange and Andrée to his *dominio*—or at least to his particular concept of domination. He refuses to reëxamine his methods or his point of view even when he learns that Thérèse Pantevin, entirely broken under the double burden of misdirected religion and misguided love, goes completely mad. Costals really does not understand the implications of her madness, nor does he feel the slightest pangs of remorse for having pushed her toward insanity. He senses that Thérèse suffers less from a genuine mental illness than from the common malady of being "different." Costals' logic is odd: he translates the whole matter into a new context that perhaps best suits his well-being. Because Thérèse is different from the crowd and an alien in her provincial milieu, she meets a fate generally familiar to artists like Costals. Without the strength of Costals, however, she is defeated by society—the crowd. More characteristically, Costals notes that he is indifferent to her madness and suffering; he would pray for her if he had a faith that would give meaning to prayer. I believe that Montherlant tries to create a believable man in Costals, but Costals' egocentricity is so overwhelming, his sense of compassion so far removed from the human scope, that he ceases to be believable. Montherlant's irony is too forced, and Costals' mind is too remote from the fringes of normalcy. In a real sense Costals is himself a psychopath.

Andrée Hacquebaut in *Pitié pour les femmes* dares to re-emerge from her provincial world of Saint-Léonard for yet another encounter with Costals. In one sense she is less disturbing than Thérèse, for her masochism parallels Costals' sadism. It is this bizarre balance of masochism-sadism that tends to reduce the impact of either portion of the balance. In his Paris studio, Costals intends to demonstrate, with Solange as unseen witness, the appalling lengths to which some women will go when driven by their emotions; he also intends to portray the meaning of his indifference to such emotions. But I am disturbed by Costals' use of the word indifference, for it implies negation, non-action. Yet for Costals indifference is an instrument of action, whether it take the form of a letter or a meeting. His indifference, furthermore, calls for a strange form of revenge directed against Andrée, a revenge that Solange witnesses. Costals carefully plans his pseudo-scientific experiment in order to punish Andrée for loving him. Montherlant, of course, describes the experimentation as the automatic gesture of syncretic man capable of emotions but totally indifferent to them.[17] It is well to remember, however, that Montherlant admits to Costals' lack of humanity toward others; he does not deny his amorality.

Costals' inhuman and grotesque plan to humiliate Andrée is described in a meaningless way. The sense of their conversation in the studio is unenlightened, and it seems to be merely a continuation of their exchange of letters. Their attempts to communicate—although I am not sure that Costals wishes to communicate—lead to an absurd void and finally to a sort of destruction without purpose. Like a child whose natural cruelty encourages him to dare all the possibilities of physical and mental outrage of another, Costals plays the rôle of a child-like man: he anticipates some form of retaliation. Does Andrée have a gun? Will she slap him? Rather than avoid retaliation by moving away from Andrée, Costals places himself closer to her—like a matador. He wants to emulate matadors who dare the animal by taking a more dangerous position. But there is no retaliation, and Costals gives a final gesture of his disdain. Seeing Andrée to the door, he thinks of his broken doorbell which rarely rings when the door is opened from the inside. It suddenly occurs to him that this time, if the bell rings, he will kiss Andrée; it does not ring, and he sees her out without kissing her. Are we dealing with *dominio* or with mental disturbance? Montherlant's monster is probably closer to the human animal than we would like to think. After Andrée has gone, Costals admits to Solange, who has heard the conversation, that he hopes Andrée will commit suicide to put an end to their relationship; he is far more concerned with being rid of a tiresome person who imposes herself on his life.

Neither suicide nor silence remove Andrée from the novel, however. If Andrée uses neither a well-deserved pistol nor a well-directed slap during her visit to Costals' studio, she has her revenge in the form of a letter—her only weapon, in fact—intended to destroy what she thinks is Costals' only power, his masculinity. Her letter addressed to Costals is chaotically composed of accusations of homosexuality, and she compares him with Charlus, the Proustian homosexual she had read about during her unintelligent voyage into French literature: Andrée always wishes her weapon to be of first quality. Costals, still wrapped in his indifference, passes off the attack as simply another evidence of the automatic reaction of women. Costals classifies her automatic response to his sadism as reaction no. 174, as opposed to woman's desperation in religion, to recall Thérèse Pantevin, which is reaction no. 89. He cites three truths concerning himself and women. First, he claims never to have been insulted by a pretty woman; second, Andrée should become a literary critic because she cannot see truth when it is before her eyes; and third, he must always destroy the "evidence" of his life by continually replacing old masks for new ones. His intellectual attitude toward women, for example, must not be confused with his physical attraction to them. He does not reveal his findings to Andrée, but rather to his friend Pailhès. While Costals spends his time in psychological self-analysis, Andrée spends hers by writing to her friends in Paris to find out why they had never told her of Costals' homosexuality.

The novel's emphasis is partly directed to Andrée's revenge, partly to a curious non sequitur of her reasoning: despite her questioning and accusation, she still confesses to a lingering love for Costals and still thinks of marriage with him. For Montherlant, of course, a non sequitur is a part of logic. Andrée's dream world is such that she can first try to defeat Costals and then marry him; of course, she knows that Costals is not a homosexual. Despite the inanity of her method of revenge and the absurdity of her intention, her objective is seen by Montherlant to be a normal one. Her masochism is little different from Thérèse's self-punishment; her intellectualism, completely unconvincing and shallow, is a pitiful attempt to match that of Costals. But Andrée could have meaning for Costals only if she ceased to be clothed in civilization's false values, and only if she became a sensual object entirely devoid of thought.

Parenthetically, one may wish to ask Montherlant why he has never created a fully defined prototype of the primitive woman his primitive man seems to require. Such a person never really emerges clearly from his work—save perhaps Rhadidja in *Les Lépreuses,* Ram in *L'Histoire d'amour de "La Rose de sable,"* and women of the poems in *Encore un instant de bonheur.* They, together with Douce of *Le Songe,* are too briefly described, too remote from the author's focus.

Montherlant directs a more leisurely attention to Solange Dandillot. Costals' eager attraction to her is largely based upon his belief that Solange is sane, not in love with him, and not drawn to him through false intellectualism. It is evident, however, that even in his casual relationship with Solange he walks softly and dreads the moment when she, like all women he has known, will make a misstep in the unwanted direction of sentimentality. In a remark that forecasts the instability of their relationship, he reveals that Solange has neither taste nor aptitude for anything. But the remark suggests a primitive nature he admires, and he is drawn to her naturalness. According to Costals she possesses qualities usually associated with the women of Southern France—the Mediterranean world—women of innocence and naïveté. Although she has no faith, she adheres to the Church's formalities and attends Mass regularly; but because she stopped going to confession she is intelligent, according to Costals. She has long ceased to communicate with her parents, to be able to cry, or to offer human warmth in her relationships with adults or children. In her differentness she is entirely appealing to the artist. Unlike Andrée, who claims to understand literature, Solange admits to being lost in it; novels and poetry have no meaning for her. Again, however, Montherlant creates his familiar non sequitur: he describes her as an exaggerated rightist in politics without defining why or how.

As she is traced in *Pitié pour les femmes* Solange seems never to have emerged from a cocoon of adolescence. Pallid and passive, she moves without experience and certainly without spirit in Costals' world. In this case history, one wonders if there can be any communication between the two. While she is not a primitive—precisely because of her bourgeois background—she stands nevertheless in the periphery of the primitive and is then able to give Costals his unique pleasure. Rather, she is a fit student whom he can train. It is clearly Costals' intention to mold her character so that she may fit into his concept of womanhood, to divorce her as quickly as possible from the devastatingly ruinous influence of her middle-class background, to draw out the primitive nature he assumes always to move just below the surface, and to suppress all touches of intellectualism that may have twisted her mind. To a certain degree her character is already preformed. It is far easier for Solange to enter the world of Costals' chaos and nihilism than it was for Andrée; indeed, Solange is defenseless against any force louder than a whisper.

Solange is not totally incapable of love: she simply does not know what it is when she meets it. Costals remains determined to avoid the obligations that love imposes and to remain entirely within the sphere of carnal love. Once Solange does discover that she is in love, she has the intuitive power to sense her danger although not the intelligence to foresee her tragedy. Doomed, she accepts rather too passively the rôle of a woman irrevocably bound to a lover. She begins to accept his attitudes on all subjects. After Andrée's visit to Costals' studio, Solange, who is a witness, shows no anger; rather, she displays a vast incomprehension of what takes place. She is not shocked when Costals shows her some of Andrée's letters, but she does ask him why he continues to write to such women. Costals' answer, as usual, evades the issue.

Costals becomes more cunning in his relationship with Solange. He persuades himself that he wishes to bring evil to this new victim, and he gradually directs his sadism toward her, seemingly without great motivation. He pities her because she is his victim, and he is suddenly inspired to put their relationship to the use of literature. He already visualizes how, in some future novel characterization, he can use her teeth, which remind him of the teeth of a decapitated sheep. Solange, as well as the other women, will serve as a sort of literary bloodbank for Costals' art, and his art will prosper because of his experimentations. It becomes increasingly apparent that life for Costals is a progression of events meant to serve his talent, which he deems unique. Only the literary work—never humanity—can survive the passage of time. Gratuitously, he admits to Solange a further contribution that he can make to the world: the pleasure he gives to women.

Among the members of the long parade of people meant to serve literature are Solange's parents. It goes without saying that Costals, invited to dinner to meet M. and Mme Dandillot, looks forward to the evening with considerable misgivings and dread. First, such a dinner symbolizes Solange's love; second, her parents, like all parents, are forever the disappointing monsters of human mediocrity. Costals finds that Mme Dandillot's bearing reminds him of a policeman's horse, and he notes that she forever converses on the level of the absurd. He studies carefully this obvious enemy who already thinks of him as a son-in-law; he detests the basic dishonesty of Mme Dandillot's game. Costals' greater concentration, however, is fixed upon M. Dandillot, because he senses the possibility of some form of meaningful communication with him. In a real sense the conversation between M. Dandillot and Costals represents the first and only exchange of ideas in the four novels. As a former sportsman and director of athletics—by implication he is an aging hero of a worthwhile past—M. Dandillot gives evidence of his quality of mind and of his natural intelligence; he is also wary of certain bourgeois values and has rejected, for example, the Legion of Honor. More to the point, he is dying of cancer and is anxious to communicate with someone worthy, for neither his wife nor daughter has ever understood him. In their sharing of mutual interest it is apparent that M. Dandillot is an older Costals; the two character portrayals have a singular oneness. But M. Dandillot has pushed farther into life, for he has married and assumed marriage's responsibilities. He is seen, then, as the man Costals might be were he to give up his liberty. Their conversation is at a high level, at least from Costals' point of view. They discuss suicide as an escape from life as well as the advantages of sleep—as a preliminary escape from life. Indeed, Costals discusses the several ways of committing suicide.

Motherlant creates M. Dandillot to show how an intelligent man can go wrong. M. Dandillot's life has been a wasteland of conformity: first, a marriage without love, and second, a social existence in a meaningless vacuum because it has adhered to his wife's concepts. He has done his duty without recompense of any sort. At the end of his life his habit of conformity robs him even of a way out, for his milieu objects to suicide, and he cannot spend his last days in a clinic, if only to capture even in that narrow world a final glimpse of something different. Both M. Dandillot and Costals have the same egotism, although it guides M. Dandillot toward oblivion and Costals toward chaos.

Characteristically, Costals gently denounces the only meaningful relationship he has had thus far. When M. Dandillot regrets that he has met Costals so close to the end of his life, Costals retorts that under normal circumstances they never could have been friends because M. Dandillot would have bored him. Despite their oneness, they are precise contrasts, of course. Costals cannot understand M. Dandillot's "weaknesses"; he especially cannot understand how M. Dandillot could have committed the spiritual "suicide" of marriage. But the younger man is disturbed primarily because he thinks he is looking at himself: rather, he is looking at a version of himself in the form of M. Dandillot, and he plans to avoid such a trap. Does M. Dandillot have a faith? He does mention it, but he refuses to conceive of a Catholic in his milieu and is visibly upset that Costals may be a practicing Catholic. He finally asks Costals about his position. When Costals answers that he has none, M. Dandillot exclaims: "Bonheur de l'homme sans Dieu!"—happiness of man without God. Of course, his exclamation is a deformation of Pascal's "Misère de l'homme sans Dieu"—wretchedness of man without God. Indeed, their conversation ends on this strange note of M. Dandillot's gratitude.

The parenthetical depiction of M. Dandillot underlines the curious emphases of Montherlant's novels. I have already pointed out such literary swerving in *Les Célibataires:* the change of emphasis from Elie to Léon, together with the briefer portrayal of Octave. An examination of the first two novels of the tetralogy shows that they begin with Thérèse, continue primarily with Andrée, but they end with Solange. M. Dandillot's appearance at the end of *Pitié pour les femmes* is in balance with Solange's appearance at the conclusion of *Les Jeunes Filles.* In the last two novels the author's focus is fixed more directly upon Costals and Solange.

3. LE DÉMON DU BIEN (DEMON OF GOOD). If Montherlant is to be treated as author of a "thesis novel"—the thesis of the artist's need for an extraordinary elevation beyond fundamental moral obligations—he is at his best in *Le Démon du bien* where he achieves

an essential high point in the development of that thesis. As in the first two novels, Costals still seeks to defend his freedom in the name of his creativity; he is still on the defensive against any false influences others may wish to impose; he is still convinced that marriage and love are inevitable obstacles to grandeur. In the first novels, nonetheless, Costals is a thoroughly convinced young man: his weakness and loss of direction, despite his "proofs" of his great experiment, are seen only through our eyes, providing, of course, we choose to reject Costals' values. Surprisingly, Costals becomes more human, more believable in *Le Démon du bien* because he begins to feel unsure of himself, to doubt some of his values, and to tend to wish for a new kind of experience.

Costals is neither rejuvenated nor changed in the third novel; the modifications in his character develop gradually. In constant fear of Solange's love for him, he lectures her at length about false bourgeois values. Yet his arguments begin to take on a strident tone, they more closely resemble irrationality, and his actions become increasingly more frenetic. Finally, he wavers between the idea of marriage with Solange—as a sort of resignation—and the continuance of their affair as it is. He can never pinpoint his feelings, however, and can never reach a precise conclusion within his own mind. He is as cruel to Solange as before, although his cruelty does not possess the meaningless sadism directed toward Thérèse and Andrée. Now his cruelty more clearly stems from his lack of emotional stability, and is less calculated. The nobility of his *dominio* is more reduced, the grandeur of the artist defending a way of life seems genuinely absurd, and the man begins to emerge on the level of human understanding. For the first time he elicits our sympathy.

The more Costals reveals his views to Solange, the more he makes evident his humanity, which is reason enough for her to fall more deeply in love with him. He creates his own monster. *Le Démon du bien* does not become suddenly a love story, of course, for Montherlant directs his attention to Costals' protestations, and in doing so, he permits Solange to fall back into the shadows of the novel. Her few words, steeped in a continuing naïveté, lack any depth of meaning. Why is her reaction to Costals so completely banal? Why is she so unlike Andrée, who at least manages to spray venom in the direction of her torturer? Of course, Solange is less intelligent than Andrée; more to the point, she is guided toward a protectionism of her few bourgeois values. In her milieu marriage must be the single expression of love; children are the necessary manifestations of love. There is no other path to follow, for it is the only one that guarantees solidity and future generations. She is unaware of the waste within her own family: she has never understood her father's isolation or her mother's vacuousness, or even her own futility as a human. Costals, acutely aware of the dangers of human ties, fights against what Solange represents and not against Solange herself.

As Costals approaches the idea of marriage, he is no closer to the idea of human decency. Marriage with Solange, creating normalcy for her, would perhaps give him some temporary peace of mind; but intellectually he fears such a solution and realizes that her normalcy would mean his personal and artistic defeat. Typically, his arguments move from the human level to the level of "literature": To what extent will his art suffer if he makes such a sacrifice? His marriage to Solange would not result from a concept of social responsibility—his son Philippe serves as an example of his lack of responsibility. Rather, marriage would be inspired by a simple wish to make her happy, to offer her the gift of his esteem. Nonetheless, the sense of giving, or of sacrificing, annoys Costals, for obligation is at the root of giving, and obligation is the larger portion of man's chaos. In brief moments of exaltation he believes that marriage would demonstrate his capacity for grandeur, because it would serve literature. In a somewhat Cornelian concept, marriage would also permit him to know the sense of duty. Never the consequence of love, marriage must be a cerebral calculation. Just as we know that in Cornelian tragedy duty will inevitably have dominion over the passions, we know that in Montherlantian works the passions will have dominion over duty: the poles are completely reversed.

To formulate the psychology of his future literature, Costals notes all reactions—both his and Solange's—with the care of a scientist. Solange is little more than an object of his experiment; his "esteem" for her is entirely sensual and carnal, and his sense of duty is a temporary phase of an awkward mood. His dignity is barely visible. What Costals does have is a fear of life, and it is a cowardice he cannot define. He becomes a man of hypotheses unable to arrive at valid conclusions. Pursuing the hypothesis of marriage, Costals imposes a list of conditions that seem ludicrous, but Mme Dandillot, desperately wishing to see her daughter settled, accepts all of them. With the conditions accepted, however,

Costals still continues to vacillate. Whenever his hypothesis approaches reality—he is even afraid of the word "fiancé"—he makes a frenetic retreat. What might have ennobled his literature assumes proportions too large for him to swallow. If Costals the man of letters becomes afraid of his own experimentations, Costals the psychologist can no longer bear to participate in his own science. His fright drives him to consult a lawyer, for Costals wants a legal document facilitating divorce: France's stringent laws protecting the innocent wife are too much for him.

There is escape from his chaos of indecision. First, there is sleep—a common theme in Montherlant's work—and Costals resorts to using sleeping pills; he is not yet ready for the final escape of actual suicide. He flees to Genoa—to write, of course, but surely to remove himself from Solange's world. He writes to Solange that he continues to use her in his literature. Solange, with expected stupidity—or is she simply a girl in love?—accepts his invitation to join him for two weeks in Italy. The invitation is meant to provide a moment of happiness for them, for Costals makes it clear that he prefers to drop the matter of marriage. One example of Montherlant's excellent grasp of psychological verisimilitude is contained in his description of the Genoa railway station as Costals waits for Solange's train. With only six minutes left, Costals is suddenly attracted to a strange woman on the platform. During his last minutes of freedom he loses himself in a sexual frenzy, rapidly replaced by a furious frustration at not being able to meet and make love to the stranger: at that moment he realizes that Solange's visit is a mistake, an obstacle to his freedom. When Solange steps down from her train, she is given a perfunctory kiss—"un baiser de mari." Of course, the scene on the station platform reduces Solange's visit to an absurd matter of no consequence, for Costals has a new determination to remain free, to live for his work, and to know all of the sensuality, primitive and carnal, that strangers afford him.

Out of compassion, Costals tries to make Solange's visit happy; but he rejects brief thoughts of marriage. Solange submits to Costals' "love," but she remains a faded object who spends most of her time listening to Costals' soliloquies on the nature of man and woman. He longs for the aftermath of the Genoa tryst when Solange's love will perhaps have turned into hatred. But suddenly he proposes again the "if" of marriage: Would she willingly consent to an abortion if she became pregnant after marriage? Her affirmative answer—by this time she is willing to play his game without question—underscores not so much her despair but rather her passiveness. By the same token, Costals' *dominio* is temporarily saved. After Solange leaves for Paris, Costals spends his time sleeping.

Montherlant prefaces *Le Démon du bien* with a brief fantasy in which someone—we assume that it is Montherlant—looks carefully at Costals, his "dear colleague," orating before Solange. In a postscript to the novel Montherlant adds the manuscript "Iblis," sent to Costals by one of his literary friends. It is in the form of a dialogue between Iblis (Lucifer) and Jesus concerning the rôle of the demon who seeks to do evil but who gains no satisfaction from it. Montherlant's intention is to point out both the good and the evil that must exist in a man such as Costals. Once liberated from marriage, a social restraint of bourgeois society, he is free to devote himself with appropriate abandon to his creative and sensual nature. The novel ends with a parody of Genesis, in which Costals devotes himself first to the creation of his art and then to worldly pleasures—in measures of time. Costals hence emerges now as a sort of "divine creator" endowed with both good and evil. On the seventy-first day of his "creation"—dating from the time of Solange's departure for Paris—he, too, leaves for Paris.

4. LES LÉPREUSES (THE LEPERS). The definitions of psychological chaos already described in *Les Jeunes Filles,* plus the amorality of *Pitié pour les femmes* and of *Le Démon du bien,* ending with the parody of creation, would seem entirely sufficient to define Montherlant's novelistic purposes. Yet he adds a final work, *Les Lépreuses* (1939), which serves to add nothing new to the experimentation; rather, it is a postlude that carries Costals' characterization to new lengths, though not to greater meaningfulness. It is a surprising work, for it gratuitously follows the path of Costals' new freedom. Traveling in Morocco, he meets a former mistress—the primitive Rhadidja—with whom he at last finds a freedom founded on indifference, a sensuous love devoid of society's obligations. Also somewhat gratutitously, Costals believes that he contracts leprosy from her. But this demon of good and evil finds that leprosy is rather less tragic than it is imposing: it is at least a malady on a grand scale and has about it the quality of grandeur.

Returning to Paris for a thorough medical examination, Costals briefly turns to the fringes of religion and to the edge of his former life with Solange. Costals notes, however, that he takes religion as one takes quinine. As for Solange, she serves as a refuge of sorts, and she can scarcely understand why. Of course, Costals holds it against her precisely because she is a refuge, and he recalls that she has harmed him in their past relationship.[18] His attitude reflects a typical Montherlantian reversal: out of sadism Costals tells her of his leprosy and explains in detail how he got it. When he learns later that he does not have the disease, he refuses at first to wipe away such grandeur. He also rediscovers Solange's faded quality and realizes to his horror that she has become another Andrée. At this point Solange disappears from the novel, for her usefulness to Costals evaporates.

We have come full circle as Costals sees Andrée in Solange. Curiously, it is Andrée Hacquebaut's letter to Costals, which appears in the novel's "Epilogue," that sums up the utter nihilism of Costals' world. Andrée understands that Costals' multiple attitudes and his many poses are meaningless: she sees him finally as a static creature without intelligence.[19] Andrée, at least, penetrates Costals' "mystery" even if only in a momentary enlightenment. Where Solange-as-object is never able to perceive Costals clearly, Andrée at last manages to capture and identify his utter stupidity, his bestiality, the pointlessness of his devotion to literature as an exclusive way of life. The bourgeois Solange—who in the meantime has married an engineer, without love—satisfies the requirements of her caste. The novel ends with an appendix of aphorisms concerning the ignoble character of women in a society of men.

V *Evaluation of the Tetralogy*

In order to grasp the full sense of the four novels comprising the tetralogy, it is unfortunately necessary to read them in their entirety and in proper sequence. My own conclusion is that Montherlant has not created in the tetralogy a monumental study of women. On the contrary, he has carefully selected certain types of women—Thérèse, Andrée, Solange, and even Rhadidja—who represent unusual or abnormal human traits. The experimentation is therefore prejudiced in advance. But Montherlant's focus is on Costals rather than on the women; indeed, *Les Jeunes Filles* is devoted to a psychological study of a young man, part artist, part devil, part god, and part Hamlet. He is doomed to the hell of his self-imposed isolation. Only M. Dandillot, as a brief parenthesis in the novel's development, elicits our sympathy. He is a Costals that might have been, and he is a mirror-image of the artist.

What strikes me as being worthy of mention is Montherlant's apparent inability to be concise in the tetralogy. His repetitions, while partly necessary to the development of character portrayals, become in time altogether too frequent, and often they do not add expected insights. The author runs considerable risk in piling repetition upon repetition, evidence upon evidence: his situations become tiresome, his depiction of sadism less authentic, and his originality lost in verbalizing. Of course, the four novels would make a superb single novel. Montherlant lacks in these novels an economy of language and a discipline of style, for while the works do demonstrate his capacity for brilliant language, they reveal it in scattered form. Finally, the author has the tendency to move from the serious to the ludicrous without transitions: the leprosy episode, for example, adds little scope to the novels. A final commentary on Solange is written in boxing terms. Montherlant does admire the Chaplinesque sort of humor, but he does not always use it with good grace.

Yet readers with patience will enjoy *Les Jeunes Filles:* its language makes the effort worthwhile, and its psychological experimentation can be fascinating. For the serious student of Montherlant's work, the tetralogy is an absolute necessity, for it permits a view of syncretic man moving in a specific milieu toward his final destruction.

VI Le Chaos et la nuit (Chaos and Night)

A considerable gap of time lies between *Les Jeunes Filles* and Montherlant's latest novel, *Le Chaos et la nuit* (1963). Of course, during the long hiatus he had turned to theater, which I think is his preferred genre. One might expect that *Le Chaos et la nuit* would contain evidence of dramatic perfection as well as a perfection of character analysis; one might also look forward to a culmination of a novelist technique, or at least to the absence of a loose construction—for I consider his earlier novels imperfectly designed. To be sure, *Le Chaos et la nuit* does have a tighter construction than *Les Célibataires* or *Les Jeunes Filles,* and both language and plot are more disciplined. By the same token, he does not swerve radically from his familiar themes or focus, although in the last novel there is a different use of theme and what one might term a different level of focus. Bullfighting, with all of its symbolism put to many uses by Montherlant, still remains as a portion of the mystique of Rome, but now it is transformed into a negative symbolism, into a nihilism, and it is seen through the eyes of a man lost in his own helplessness and hopelessness. Like *La Petite Infante de Castille, Le Chaos et la nuit* is the antidote for the lyric *Les Bestiaires;* the opposite side of the mystique is visible.

In *Le Chaos et la nuit* we are concerned with the title's implications: man's chaos, which is his life, and man's night, which is his meaningless death. Instead of the lyric joys expressed in the early novels, instead of a dogged pursuit for a meaningful life—Alban de Bricoule in *Le Songe,* for example—the work stands as an antithesis. Celestino is the reverse of Alban, and he is more directly related to Léon de Coantré of *Les Célibataires.* A non-hero like Léon, Celestino is engulfed in an anarchy more personal than political, which translates itself into despair. But his struggle with fate is really not in question, for Celestino is already at the novel's beginning the skeleton of his former self. Certainly, the theme of self-destruction, already evident in *Les Célibataires* and implied in *Les Jeunes Filles*, becomes the dominant theme of the novel. Unlike Léon, however, whose wish for death is an unconscious movement, Celestino is more aware of his rapid plunge toward death. He is not intellectually aware of the inevitability of death: it simply happens. Yet there is an energy in Celestino's decline, an energy that Léon does not possess. Trained to be an anarchist, Celestino remains one to the end, using his few remaining powers to prepare the way for his death; as far as the novel is concerned, his anarchy is personal and psychological. Always balanced with his energy is his penchant for defeat. Like Léon and Costals, Celestino permits sleep to replace action, and words—torrents of words—to replace deeds. In his downward plunge toward annihilation Celestino senses intuitively the need to be rid of the unnecessary "baggage" of life, whether friends, relatives, or even ideas. Again, a thinly defined dignity—the sense of caste, the meaningless title—leaves Léon de Coantré in a state of inaction. A similar grandeur, although not one of caste, lies at the base of Celestino's manhood. First, he is Spanish; second, he is an acknowledged former anarchist; and finally, he is right. He is a non-hero in a real sense because he never comes to grips with his life in any intellectual way and never acts logically.

Le Chaos et la nuit is a brief novel divided into two parts. The first part describes Celestino's life as an exile in Paris, where he lives with his daughter Pascualita. Their life together is simple, their comfort is maintained through a small income, and their isolation, especially from Frenchmen, is thorough. The second part of the novel concerns their return to Spain to share in a family will, a return made difficult because of Celestino's former political activity. Only the possibility of arrest offers a threat to Celestino during the novel's progression.

In Paris the aging Spanish Republican is forced to live in a milieu he finds totally incomprehensible and alien. He is surrounded by few links to his Spanish world. Pascualita in one sense serves as a link, but communication between father and daughter is limited at best, and at the age of twenty Pascualita seems a faded woman of little importance. While a dutiful daughter, she lacks intellectual insights, and she appears as a soulless creature, at least during the first part of the novel. Celestino does have a few friends outside of his home; they include Ruiz, Pineda, and his business advisor Moragas. Now, years after the Revolution, they are meaningless links, for their Spain has disappeared. What they still have is a link to a concept of Spain, a memory of a Spain transformed by faulty memory into a non-existent land. But Spain is seen only through Celestino's eyes, for his friends do not stand out in relief: Montherlant again creates a soliloquy novel in which only Celestino's speech and thoughts dominate. The words of Ruiz, Pineda, and Moragas have little bearing, since they serve only as instruments of the drama. For this reason, I believe that *Le Chaos et la nuit* would have made a better play because it displays the strengths of Montherlant's dramatic technique; it also proves the author's ability to use discipline in the novel, a discipline undoubtedly acquired during his long career as playwright.

In this drama-novel, Celestino is an anarchist who has failed politically. His years in Paris as a refugee are years of failure and frustration on an entirely personal scale. Montherlant does not concern himself with studying either anarchy as a political phenomenon or Spain's historical Revolution; he studies, rather, the inner anarchy, or chaos, of Celestino's mind, and it is a study of the effect of such anarchy after years of deadly inaction. Celestino's brain, never proposed as capable of sound logic, seems washed and devoid of purpose. As a consequence, his concern for the past—for a Spain that was and for a Spain that might have been—is clothed in complete darkness. All of his arguments and his expressed hatreds are as meaningless as he is himself; they are as fictional as his sense of action. Since his own chaos is the subject of the novel, it is pointless to look for political meaning: there are no political issues whatsoever in the work. The mystique of Rome is in *Le Chaos et la nuit,* but it is transformed into a mystique of Spain.

But France, Spain, the Falangists, and even national purpose serve only as futile backdrops and usually as unconvincing references for Celestino's private hell. Celestino does talk about the Generation of 1898, for example, a generation of Spanish intellectuals concerned because of Spain's decline, but he has no awareness of what the problems were: yet Spain's decline feeds his bitterness and discontent. His anti-Americanism is another toy of his hatred: he is anti-American because a "proper" Spaniard should be. But he is also anti-French because France is always the traditional enemy, although he hates France primarily because it has given him shelter and thereby posed an obligation. And Spain itself, in Celestino's mad mind, is also the enemy because it continues to go downhill and to submit to insidious foreign influence; it has made the mistake of adopting the errors of Western progress, especially a Northern progress. In point of fact, Celestino's Spain has never existed and will never exist. The mentally impoverished Celestino—at least as he is depicted by Montherlant—is a sort of mindless Don Quixote in search of an ideal Spain.

Celestino's grandeur—if grandeur correctly describes Celestino—is his Spanishness; yet his Spanishness is clearly an aberration pushing him toward self-destruction. In the first part of the novel he seems bent upon some unknown goal requiring him to slough off his last links with Spain. Breaking off with Ruiz and Pineda, he has only Moragas left. His insistent movement to break with society is symbolized in a ludicrous scene in a Paris park: he scatters pigeons to annoy the people sitting nearby. Without logic, his grandeur is also his stance, that of a Romanized and romanticized Spaniard of chimerical powers. Celestino is unbending and utterly humorless, although he still has a self-sufficiency that stems from his mindlessness. He also displays the mental rigidity usually associated with old age, together with an enormous egotism and a flock of calculated manias; his principal mania is that of being contrary for no reason. This bizarre concept of grandeur is perhaps more immediately visible in the second part of the novel in which Celestino finally becomes a non-Spaniard in an unheard-of Spain.

The alien Celestino finds himself at odds with the real Spain and constantly contrasts what he assumes to be his genuine Spanishness with the "false" Spanishness that surrounds him in Madrid. This contrast is made most evident when he avidly returns to the bullring—symbol of a cult and the purity of Spain. There, amidst the spectators, Celestino finds that the corrida has become sloppy, commercialized, and popularized; the noble cult, as it is described in *Les Bestiaires,* is now a watered version of its former beauty and power. Like Alban of *Les Bestiaires,* he notes that the public is now a hideous mob unworthy to participate in the drama of the cult. Revolted by the experience at the corrida, Celestino characteristically divorces the cult from his life, just as he subtracts from it his friends Ruiz and Pineda.

Similarly, he breaks with Pascualita, especially as she emerges, in Madrid, as having a grandeur of her own. In his mind, of course, Celestino is right: Pascualita in Spain begins to bloom among her countrymen, and, obviously more rational than her father, she absorbs Spain as it is, although her acceptance of it proves her mediocrity in her father's eyes. Celestino's increasing aloneness in an alien nightmare, his destruction of links, all prepare the way for his end. He suggests Léon de Coantré, as I have remarked, although Léon's self-destruction and aloneness result from a different force. Celestino's rage to cast off life, especially in terms of human relationships, stems from willful acts—hence, a sort of energy—however irrational and psychopathic they are.

His death in his hotel room is scarcely surprising; it is no more so than Léon's death in the cottage at Fréville. It precedes by minutes the arrival of the police to arrest him as an enemy of the state. Léon's death, however, appears in a more normal and natural progression of events; the addition of a political element at the conclusion of *Le Chaos et la nuit* seems unjustified. To be sure, Celestino through death escapes the police, but not defiantly or by dint of a last movement of energy. It is the novel's conclusion that troubles me the most. Montherlant seems again to have twisted the sense of his character in the last few moments of his life—but without his being able to change Celestino or add new meaning to the novel. I also find that his death is too "philosophical" to be real, his thoughts finally too noble and too rational, even too grandiose, to be convincing. At the novel's conclusion, Celestino is suddenly transformed from a figure of chaos into a commentator of chaos.

VII *A Note on the Future of Montherlant's Novels*

It is impossible now to forecast with accuracy the public's reaction to the Montherlantian novel. Montherlant, while interested in the future of his work, is equally unsure of the place his novels will have in the history of French literature. A battle-weary, sophisticated public will probably reject *Le Songe* if it understands the work as a "war novel," which it is not. *Les Bestiaires* has an assured public, at least among the aficionados of the bullring: it is a superbly wrought description of a pagan-Christian cult. At best, its incantations are poetic and they will continue to have appeal for youth in quest of personal freedom. Similarly, *Les Olympiques* and *La Petite Infante de Castille,* lying at the edge of the novel's form, will draw readers from among youths.

Les Célibataires, despite its nineteenth-century atmosphere, will interest those seriously drawn to Montherlant's later concern for studies of the human condition. By the same token, *Le Chaos et la nuit,* with a novelistic structure surpassing that of his earlier works, studies a phase of the author's syncretic man and does it superbly for the most part. Montherlant's reputation—or his notoriety—may well be founded on the tetralogy of *Les Jeunes Filles,* however; I find this possibility unfortunate. The four novels are controversial, of course, primarily because it is not aways easy to determine Montherlant's emphasis, which strays from women in general to women in particular, and from women to Costals. Of course, once it becomes clear that his emphasis is directed toward Costals, the novels begin to have meaning and certainly value in terms of psychological reality. Students should look with care through the author's magnifying glass at the massive experiment he proposes.

Montherlant's novels offer something more than psychological analysis. They are the showcase, together with his essays, of a brilliant style that often surpasses that of the best of twentieth-century writers. At his best, he creates a successful marriage between thought and language, especially in *Les Célibataires* and *Le Chaos et la nuit,* which gives evidence of his ability to control poetic prose.

The novel is perhaps not Montherlant's favorite genre, for despite his sense of poetry, of language, and especially of character analysis in depth, his novels lack the exacting discipline the genre requires. Montherlant's natural tendency to overstate has too great freedom in the novel, a genre without precise limits. He finds his discipline in drama, and he never loses from view the most necessary instrument of drama: psychological truth.

CHAPTER 4

Drama of Contemporary Theme

I *A Note on Chronology*

THE plays that Montherlant devotes to contemporary dramatic themes have at first sight an erratic chronology. *L'Exil,* never produced, was written in 1914 and published in 1929; it precedes by twenty-six years his *Port-Royal.* The second play devoted to a contemporary theme, *Fils de personne,* was written and unproduced in 1943 during the German occupation of France. *Un Incompris,* a one-act play designed by Montherlant to balance *Fils de personne* on the same theatrical program, had to be abandoned because of a newly imposed German curfew. Not until 1948 did he create *Demain il fera jour* as sequel to *Fils de personne*—and *Demain il fera jour* was produced only the following year. Finally, *Celles qu'on prend dans ses bras,* written in 1949, was produced in 1950. Curiously, *La Ville dont le prince est un enfant,* published in 1951, is based upon the author's notes of 1913; it precedes *L'Exil,* therefore, in terms of conception, although from the point of view of dramatic expression it reveals a mature playwright.

One may make a more comprehensible grouping of the plays according to the periods they treat. *La Ville's* theme is concerned with pre-World War I; *L'Exil* more directly touches upon the period of World War I. *Fils de personne* and *Demain il fera jour* have their setting in France during the German occupation, or 1940–1941 and 1944. *Un Incompris* has no precise period, nor does it require it. Finally, *Celles qu'on prend dans ses bras* depicts the Paris of 1949.

In one sense, the plays have their parallel in the novels, beginning certainly with *Le Songe.* Yet while this portion of his total theater may thematically resemble his novels, it is essentially remote from them. In the early plays Montherlant is largely concerned with the psychology of youth inevitably in conflict with adults, and hence with an adult word of mediocrity and dishonesty. The themes of sacrifice and renunciation appear, but we are not yet involved with the full development of these themes as in such major plays as *La Reine morte* and *Port-Royal.* Only in the major plays do we note a constant link to the greater novels, especially to *Les Célibataires* and to *Le Chaos et la nuit.* Of course, *Un Incompris* and *Celles qu'on prend dans ses bras* are in balance with *Les Jeunes Filles,* although with a different and briefer focus. His plays of contemporary theme are minuscule studies of human psychology lacking the full tragedic effect of the major plays.

II La Ville dont le prince est un enfant

Montherlant typically offers his public the full documentation of this play from the time of its germination in his notes of 1913 to the time of the latter-day performances.[1] His pages include all aspects of the play's meaning, together with correspondence, explications, and information meant to shed light upon the purpose and method of his creation; his notes show his very real hesitation to have the play produced. He sensed that conservative Catholicism might be shocked more by seeing the play performed than by reading it. Despite the logic of some of his arguments, however, I feel that Montherlant may have been tossing a cold potato from one hand to the other: he protests too much and incidentally gives the erroneous impression that he is deeply concerned with Catholic opinion. His excellent drama is little more than the study of innocent adolescent love smothered by the insidious passions of an adult moving toward his own private hell. The play's portrayal of such love is neither unique nor in bad taste. I refuse, however, to call it a Catholic play, since Catholicism is never in question. Expressions of faith are absent, and Christianity's absence—or Catholicism's—does nothing to divert attention. The dramatic action does take place in a private Catholic school, but it might also take place in any secondary school peopled by adolescent boys and misguided teachers.

What is studied with fine artistic taste is the psychology of the human at odds with the code—or caste system—of his social milieu. It is natural that some sensitive adolescent boys form close and innocent attachments when they are on the threshold of manhood. André Sevrais, sixteen years old, and Serge Soubrier, age fourteen, both possess, despite the differences of their ages and backgrounds, such a delicate affection. In one sense, Sevrais speaks to Soubrier in a paternalistic manner, often with touches of condescension, and Sevrais senses the ultimate separation that age forces upon such tentative friendships. For his age Sevrais lacks maturity: the touching of blood to affirm eternal friendship suggests rather pre-adolescence. Yet Sevrais is the intellectual star of his school, and he is close to finishing his studies. I note here the faint touch of *dominio* so strongly evident in Montherlant's earlier novels. On the other hand, Montherlant suggests that Sevrais is more akin to Philippe de Presles in *L'Exil,* in which male *dominio* is not in question; indeed, he points out that the latter play should be considered a sequel to *La Ville dont le prince est un enfant.*

In *La Ville* Montherlant brings to the fore the familiar question of sacrifice. In the major portion of his work, sacrifice—or renunciation, or even spiritual suicide—is an instrument that the hero or non-hero imposes on himself; we are concerned rarely with sacrifice that results from external influences. In *La Ville* Sevrais is dismissed from his school because he is at the mercy of one of his teachers, Abbé de Pradts, who is attracted to Soubrier. Soubrier, for the most part ignorant of any rôle he may be playing, is dismissed because the headmaster, Abbé Pradeau de la Halle, finds his presence intolerable in view of De Pradts' unusual attention to the boy. At the same time the headmaster demands that De Pradts return to the disciplines of Church morality and of school authority. Dismissal of Soubrier and De Pradts' return to discipline are not sacrifices in the Montherlantian sense; neither Soubrier, Sevrais, nor De Pradts makes a sacrifice, and each is forced to obey order and morality. They have no apparent recourse to a higher power. What Montherlant does portray is a study of adolescent tragedy, especially the tragedy of the two boys. He also portrays the far more serious and dismal tragedy of De Pradts, whose seemingly innocent attraction to Soubrier is overshadowed by its meaninglessness and possible tragic consequences. It is De Pradts who draws our primary attention in this play, for he is completely out of harmony with his calling and profession, as well as with its responsibilities; he is certainly remote from his beliefs and faith. He recalls Gustave Aschenbach of Thomas Mann's *Death in Venice,* although De Pradts is an almost mindless individual moving in a spiritual void.

There is also in *La Ville* a curious anticlerical tone, although it is less pernicious than one might expect. In the first scene of the play, Soubrier—portrayed as rather devoid of understanding—is nevertheless aware that the telephone interruptions during a conversation with De Pradts reveal the teacher's capacity for petty lies. Soubrier, supposedly innocence itself, punctuates De Pradts' conversation with knowing smiles. Elsewhere, it is apparent that other boys have formed friendships as strong, as innocent, and as tentative as the friendship joining Sevrais and Soubrier; somehow these friendships go unpunished. De Pradts, for example, is aware that one student is not dismissed because his father is a member of the school's lay administration. Certainly the tone of the priestly discussions, particularly the tone of artificiality, persuades one to observe carefully the nature of rottenness at high levels—and it is a rottenness that demands its victims. The punishment of victims is never general: most victimized, of course, are the two boys. De Pradts is urged by his superior to read the biblical verse from which comes the play's title and then, as a final purge, to go to a retreat after the close of the school year. De Pradts' innocence in the entire matter is not altogether clear, but his portrayal does elicit sympathy, for he, at least, tries to struggle with his weakness. He appears in a far better light than his colleagues on the school's staff whose moralistic pronouncements sound hollow indeed, even when they are uttered *in camera.* The other teachers play a very dangerous game whose victory is guaranteed for them by their unique power. In terms of (Christian) morality, finally, only Soubrier and Sevrais achieve definition, and their future quality, to be gained by following separate paths, is implied.

Montherlant's ability to create concise dramatic structures is particularly evident in this play. *La Ville* is an example of the mature playwright's work, of course. The play's opening scene between De Pradts and Soubrier displays an adroit exposition leading the audience quickly from a clear understanding of the boys' problem on one level to a more profound comprehension, on yet another level, of De Pradts' own involvement. Montherlant is adept at handing detailed theater "business": the one-sided telephone conversation, for example, does more to reveal character than the usual stage dialogue. Again, the quotations from Racine's *Andromaque*—Sevrais is learning the rôle of Pyrrhus for the school play—lend themselves with fitting irony as counterpoint to the main action of the drama. Montherlant's forte, however, is always his ability, especially in drama, to get at the heart of the psychological problem with swiftness, intensity, and accuracy. His characters, accurately reflecting by both speech and manner their proper social milieu, act out their parts flawlessly.

La Ville, of course, is related to Montherlant's own experience: he was dismissed from the Ecole Sainte-Croix in 1912, before finishing his studies, and he has always felt a resentment toward those of his teachers who failed to understand him. But I think it is time to separate Montherlant from his work and to examine it for what it is.

III L'Exil

Montherlant calls the three-act drama *L'Exil* an expression of maternal love. Maternal love does perhaps lie at the foundation of his dramatic action, in the sense that Geneviève de Presles prevents her son Philippe from going to the war front. On the other hand, she faces World War I with heroism as a director of an ambulance group. Still, I do not see her protective refusal—overprotection, surely—as the primary sense of the play. Her smothering maternalism has long since had its negative effect and debilitating consequences on Philippe; her influence is understood at the play's beginning. At the age of eighteen, Philippe de Presles is a callow youth, accustomed to the niceties of his comfortable Parisian milieu, those of his caste, but he is nevertheless a young man on the threshold of life. His awareness of reality, of the world, has always been derived from books rather than from personal experience. If Philippe is still enveloped in a cocoon surrounded by brutal reality, he is not surprisingly a restricted romantic who tends to see war as a magnificent liberation from the cocoon. His friendship with Bernard Sénac, who does manage to get to the front, serves as a direct link to that freedom. World War I in this play, as in *Le Songe*, is both the ideal world of youth devoted to selfish ecstasies—in the Montherlantian context of the mystique of Rome—and it is at the same time a vast terrain in which adolescent friendship can attain its heights. But *L'Exil*, closely allied to *Le Songe*, is an impressionistic version of the novel which presents war only as a backdrop. Prinet is in balance with Sénac, and Alban is in balance with Philippe; war itself is absent from both the play and the novel.

L'Exil, if impressionistic, is a disciplined *Le Songe*. In the play Montherlant carefully restricts his plot to a psychological portrayal of Philippe's youthful agony of exile. There are two interpretations of the exile. First, for the greater part of the play Philippe exiles himself from his mother and seeks desperately to leave for the front in order to recreate himself, to attain a manhood from which he is withheld by his mother. The catalyst that determines his second exile—his change of mind about leaving for the front—is the return of Sénac, who is accompanied by several comrades from the trenches. Where communication between the two boys, before Sénac's departure, had been on solid footing, it ceases to exist after his return. Sénac's experiences, as well as his many new friendships made with youths outside of his caste, mature him and create his manhood. He now posseses a fresh awareness of life and a clear vision of what human relationships should be. Certainly he finds at the front—in that curious war that has no definition—a new self incapable of accepting the ideas and ideals of the past. Unfortunately Philippe, unchanged and unchanging, belongs to Sénac's rejected past. The conversation between Sénac and Philippe, a conversation that includes Sénac's friends, is a disaster. Philippe's childish brooding stands out in sharp contrast to the masculine quality of Sénac's frankness; Sénac has become indifferent to his friend Philippe. To underline further the contrast between Philippe and Sénac, the *poilus* Guerchard and Grindier, friends of Sénac despite their humble background, speak their innocent and simple language in Geneviève de Presles' comfortable livingroom. If Philippe finds their presence intolerable and Sénac's friendship with them unbearable, he is entirely conscious that they are in harmony with the times and ill at ease nowhere; Philippe knows that it is he who lacks dimension.

Portrayal in the play is explicit. Philippe's romantic yearning for the front is nothing more than an extension of his friendship for Sénac, and it is an expression of fulfillment. Sénac, and not the war, dominates his thoughts, although war seems to remain a means to a perfection. As soon as Sénac returns to the front, war no longer attracts Philippe, of course; Philippe, like Alban of *Le Songe,* has never understood war. Yet Philippe finally chooses to leave for the front—as a gesture of his maturity—to become somehow capable of communicating with his friend and to gain a soul.

It is not strange that Philippe's mother, Geneviève, demonstrates in this play some of the feminine characteristics Montherlant studies in *Les Jeunes Filles.* Unable to release her son from her grasp, she is nevertheless capable of heroism. However, Montherlant portrays her as having a trace of masculinity: perhaps because of it she can be heroic, a leader, and dominate everyone in her sphere of influence. She strikes one as being unpleasant, gratuitous, impolite, especially when she deals with her co-workers in the ambulance group. She is also entirely self-sufficient and egotistical, a woman who has become totally *engagée* in a work that is necessary to the war but meaningless to her: it is simply a thing to do and to do grandly. Philippe is little more than an object of caste; for the most part he is made to toe the line, to observe his mother's "game of war" without participating in it.

Philippe is not completely lacking in strength; he is forced, however, to assert himself not as a young man but rather as a caged victim snapping at his tormentors. In a curious scene—Geneviève receives some of her women friends—Philippe, seemingly at the mercy of social politeness, amazes the ladies with his frank statements that do not reflect the conservatism of his caste; he finally routs them with his skepticism. Of course, Philippe's enemy is always his mother; only by extension is his caste understood to be the enemy. Despite Geneviève's shortcomings, she manages to try to understand her son's desire to leave for the war. She, too, is a victim of inner conflict, for the sentimentality of her maternal instincts weakens her. Her love for Philippe, which takes the form of a battle of emotions, is something less than genuine maternal love, however, for it appears as an aberration. What is striking is the almost total absence of any form of love in *L'Exil.* What dominates in the work is the theme of friendship as one expression of human love, and Montherlant's study of Philippe's involvement with such love emerges as the play's central focus.

Whenever Motherlant treats some aspect of love, he is usually concerned at the same time with renunciation. In *Le Songe,* renunciation separates Alban from Dominique and from Prinet. In *L'Exil,* it separates Philippe from his friend Sénac. It is Philippe's obtuseness, and not Sénac's mature indifference, that creates the unchanging gulf between the two at the play's conclusion. To this sense of renunciation, of course, it is necessary to add Philippe's rejection of his mother. In final analysis, Philippe is alone, embittered, cynical, isolated from his caste, and ready to be victimized by the larger world of reality. The audience is left to accept or deny the possibility of Philippe's future quality. As in the case of so many of Montherlant's plays, each spectator must draw the action to the conclusion he wishes to see. The playwright does not always conclude for the simple reason that problems—human problems—have no facile conclusions of clear definition.

IV Fils de personne (No Man's Son) *and* Demain il fera jour (Tomorrow the Dawn)

What may indeed persuade Montherlant to suggest that *L'Exil* is a sequel to *La Ville dont le prince est un enfant* is the psychological unity of the two plays. The adolescents in both dramas are trying to cope with what must be considered as an inadequate, often corrupted world dominated by authoritarianism—adult authoritarianism seen in its worst light. The audience is left to imagine that the boys' grandeur will prevail at some indefinite time in the future and that their manhood will be sound.

Fils de personne and *Demain il fera jour* are sequel plays, for the second play gives additional meaning to the first. While the works can be read separately, they should be considered as two parts of a single work. Now Montherlant's focus shifts in large measure from a study of adolescence to a study of adult authoritarianism, to its bizarre logic or lack of it. If parental authority, for example, is the basis for dramatic action in the two plays, one might expect in balance a view of adolescence as studied in *La Ville*—the moment when adolescence is on the threshold of grandeur. But Montherlant chooses to portray a weak youngster who, in the first play, is beyond sympathy, and who, in the second play, faces an ephemeral moment of greatness.

Written and produced during the German occupation, *Fils de personne* rather vaguely reflects the period. The German occupation is incidental to the action of the plays, just as World War I is scarcely of concern in *Le Songe* or *L'Exil.* And yet the occupation indirectly affects the characters, it finally imposes itself in *Demain il fera jour,* and it causes a boy's death. In terms of dramatic effect, however, any serious upheaval would have served the same purpose. There is no German in the plays, no sense of bereavement, and no real desolation. The plays, then, transcend the problems of the moment. Of course, Nazi censorship explains in part the author's careful avoidance of making an issue of the occupation. Yet *Demain il fera jour,* written in 1948 and first produced in 1949, required no such German imprimatur. It is evident that Montherlant's goal, especially in his mature work, is to study man —man's involvement with the mystique—and not the events of a certain period. He prefers to analyze the curious function of the human animal rather than the worldly decorations that surround him.

There are but three principal characters in the plays. Georges Carrion is a successful lawyer in Marseilles in *Fils de personne.* He lives with Marie Sandoval and their son, the fourteen-year-old Gilles (Gillou) in Cannes, as yet unoccupied by the Germans; Georges Carrion commutes from Marseilles, spending weekends with his family. Gillou in this play as well as in *Demain il fera jour* is described as an illegitimate son of Georges Carrion, legally unrecognized. Most of Gillou's life has been spent away from his father; hence, his first crucial years have not been under his father's guidance or influence. It is this essential fact, of course, which explains the unformed character and the inadequacies of the boy, who is remote from his father. It also explains, in terms of Montherlantian psychology, his apparent lack of grandeur. He is closer to his mother in nature and bearing. Despite his limitations, he is adept at understanding his power over his family, a power he uses to further his own narrow purposes. Behind that power, nevertheless, there lies his vast weakness of character: he is spoiled and exceptionally immature. He has undeveloped tastes, preferring to read cheap magazines and see bad movies; effeminate because of his mother's influence, he wants to avoid military service and he worries about his hair style. But these are evidences of his debility, which stand out in sharp contrast to his father's strength and supposed dignity. If an unhealthy relationship exists between Marie Sandoval and Gillou, since her taste is scarcely more developed, a total lack of communication separates Gillou from his father.

Georges Carrion, like Ferrante of *La Reine morte,* finds himself tragically defeated in his attempt to mould his son into something resembling manhood. The audience may question Montherlant's depiction of George Carrion's dilemma, for Gillou has been "found" again by his father at the age of twelve; he has been with his father only two years. One wonders if two years are enough for Georges Carrion to create a son, to form him, and to impose a sense of grandeur that the boy can understand. Equally disconcerting is the knowledge that the boy is almost constantly with Marie Sandoval, who is a drab version of a woman and who possesses no strong sense of direction. What Georges sees in his son, however, is not so much a reflection of Marie's poor guidance, but rather a symbol of the inadequacies of an entire generation of young men. He finds tragic the fact that the future direction of France will be the responsibility of Gillou's generation. Georges

Carrion bluntly reminds Gillou that he abandoned him at birth because of his egotism, and that he must abandon him again out of defeat imposed by his son's mediocrity. At the conclusion of Georges Carrion's long speech—it resembles a soliloquy—Gillou casually picks up a magazine as if he understands, or wants to understand, nothing that his father has said. Gillou's gesture is intended to underline his own mediocrity, but Montherlant intends it to mean the mediocrity of an entire generation.

A second abandonment occurs when Marie Sandoval wishes to travel to Le Havre, ostensibly to visit her relatives but in fact to be with her lover. Too late, Gillou tries to stay behind and not cross into occupied territory. Georges adamantly refuses to change the complicated arrangements he has been able to make for his family. Gillou, in a desperate final measure, tells his father of Marie's lover; he has found out, of course, because he reads his mother's mail.

Unlike *L'Exil* and *La Ville, Fils de personne* is intended by its author to portray sacrifice and renunciation. Of course, Georges Carrion did abandon Gillou at birth. It is not always clear what the sense of his egotism is—for egotism is the reason he gives for leaving Gillou—and one can only imagine that his egotism is somehow concerned with personal liberty. He is another version of Costals, a Costals desperately afraid of responsibilities and attachments that deform. In a very real sense, Georges indulges in a partial abandonment of Gillou by establishing his family in Cannes and commuting to Marseilles: like Costals, he is not faced with observing his son's mediocrity every day. The final abandonment, as he sends Marie and Gillou off to Le Havre, stems from his final attempt to be rid of Gillou's unworthiness. The question of Georges' love for Marie simply does not exist in the plays: they have long ago ceased to have any genuine communication with each other. Yet throughout the play Georges repeatedly expresses his love for Gillou; he does make serious attempts to communicate with the boy and to help him reach his manhood. It is undoubtedly Georges' love for his son that lends tragic meaning to the plays. I am bothered, nonetheless, by the playwright's portrayal of Georges. Where he has undoubtedly wished to create a man of solid character, even a sensitive man, he has created instead—at least insofar as the audience can understand it—a pathetic individual whose heroic intentions are wiped away by awkwardness and the inability to cope with other humans. Georges lacks verisimilitude if he is meant as a symbol of grandeur, or even as a symbol of fatherhood. The real tragedy of Georges Carrion is Georges himself, who solemnly tries to create perfection without transitions.

The audience may still be drawn, however, to sympathize with Georges; it may even be sympathetically attracted to Gillou, who appears constantly, despite his obvious weaknesses, as a victim of unnecessary "sacrifice." If the term love in this context has meaning, it is not enough to affect Gillou. Georges' inability to communicate arises primarily from his unwillingness to step down from the enormously high pedestal that Montherlant has seen fit to erect for him. Ferrante on his pedestal seems right; Georges Carrion, more prosaic, strikes a ludicrous note whenever he reaches out for his family. His sacrifices, if the word can be used to describe abandonment, are more clearly associated with his own surrender.

Demain il fera jour continues *Fils de personne* without concern for hiatus. Marie, whose lover has abandoned her at Le Havre, and Gillou, now seventeen years old, live in occupied Paris. At first sight, it is apparent that Gillou has changed very little in the past few years; his father is still convinced that he is mediocre. But there is a difference in his character, a difference Montherlant traces somewhat wryly. Gillou wants to join the Resistance forces, whether through a desire for freedom or because he simply wants to assert himself. Georges finds no grandeur in Gillou's sudden yearning, however, because he is aware that Gillou's sudden courage corresponds with the arrival of the American forces in Normandy. There is a further discernible change in the play: despite his constant mention of his love for Marie and Gillou, Georges seems far colder in his relationship with his family; certainly he is more sarcastic and unbending.

Gillou plays a considerably lesser rôle in *Demain il fera jour*, for Montherlant's focus is quite constantly on Georges, as well as on the concept of his sacrifice. He permits his son to join the Resistance, in a bitter gesture of sacrifice. A messenger arrives to announce the boy's death. Marie Sandoval, thus far thoroughly mute and seemingly devoid of maternal love, cries out for Gillou; Georges, deeply affected by the news, maintains a stony silence. Marie Sandoval, rather than Georges, expresses the sense of the tragedy: she notes that Georges' sacrifices have always been manifestations of a deeply-rooted cowardice, an attempt to save himself. Georges, with characteristic blindness, replies that Gillou was "marked" from the start, and being marked, he could only be assured of a future enveloped in mediocrity. Carrying this idea to its obvious conclusion—since Georges' concern for Gillou's generation is clear—Gillou could never have offered reasonable help to the Resistance and never contributed to France's grandeur; his sacrifice is useless, and Georges' sacrifice is criminal.

Of course, the secondary implication of the play is troublesome: Gillou's contribution to France's grandeur has little bearing within the plays. Even more awkward and unjust is the implication that a young man, whether at age fourteen or at age seventeen, is incapable of radical change. We are concerned here with a Montherlantian point of view, so often expressed in his work, that grandeur lasts through age twelve; afterward, youth moves through an unpalatable adolescence toward either grandeur or mediocrity. Since Gillou is fourteen years old in the first play and lacks quality, his mediocrity is assured for all time. Georges' insistence that he loves Gillou has little conviction. Marie Sandoval's conclusion, spoken at the end of *Demain il fera jour,* appears as undeniably true. Undoubtedly, it is Georges who lacks character, who is mediocre, and who is a moral coward. His sacrifices are meaningless and carry as little conviction as his professed love.

The two plays are fascinating psychological studies, provided Montherlantian terms of reference are understood. Unfortunately, there is a static quality about both plays that disturbs audiences. Georges' lengthy speeches, unvarying and spoken as if from a lofty pedestal, are too repetitious. We are concerned with the soliloquy play—although not with classic theater—in which focus is directed to a single figure and in which supporting players are extensions of the central figure, as well as of the central focus.

V Un Incompris

Designed to be presented together with *Fils de personne* during the German occupation, *Un Incompris* (1944) had to be abandoned and deleted from the program because of the newly imposed curfew. The one-act play has never attracted a wide public, quite possibly because it is a brief work lacking in depth; yet it does offer another study of Montherlantian sacrifice. Montherlant sees his play as a form of caricature, in which the young Bruno sacrifices Rosette in the same way that Georges Carrion sacrifices Gillou.[2] I am not sure that the term caricature best describes the play's portrayals. The work more clearly suggests *Les Jeunes Filles*, novels that are scarcely meant to be caricatures, and Bruno is an impressionistic Costals. Bruno's sacrifice in *Un Incompris* seems to have little purpose: he refuses to continue an affair with Rosette—hence he sacrifices her—for the simple reason that she arrives late for a rendezvous. On the contrary, the quality of caricature seems replaced by what I prefer to call black humor, for the play is ludicrous. Montherlant is justified in commenting that Bruno is ridiculous, but he is on shakier ground when he points out that Bruno is heroic.[3] By now we are familiar with Montherlant's concept of sacrifice, a concept bound to superficial heroism in the sense that Georges Carrion is superficially heroic. Costals and Georges Carrion give evidence of an inner sickness, but Bruno has too brief a time in which to display either his heroism or his sickness.

In Montherlant's lexicon of terms, however, sacrifice need not be the result of any major phenomenon: sacrifice is a portion of man's dignity, and man must sacrifice to hold on to his self-esteem. Sacrifice, renunciation, and even self-destruction are at the heart of man's life, although in varying degrees. If understood in this sense, *Un Incompris* foretells the realities of *Les Jeunes Filles*. In its most superficial light, sacrifice may result from a misplaced comb, a casually dropped bobbypin. My remark is not meant to be facetious, of course, for similar examples are portrayed in Montherlant's psychological studies: strong motivation is not required for Montherlantian sacrifice.

The author's focus is fixed on Bruno alone rather than on the relationship between Bruno and Rosette. Nor are we to be concerned with the misunderstanding—Rosette's lateness—which motivates Bruno's sacrifice. What dominates in *Un Incompris* is Bruno's retreat first from Rosette, and then, by indifference, from his act. He is bound only to himself; he appears as removed from the play itself, as if some gauze isolated him from the full clarity of the footlights.

VI Celles qu'on prend dans ses bras

The complexity of Montherlantian psychology comes to the fore in this drama of age juxtaposed with youth. It is a mistake to emphasize the difference in age of the players, however, for the almost machinelike pivoting of attitudes and motivations scarcely depends upon the fact that Ravier is fifty-eight, that his friend

Mlle Andriot is sixty, and that Christine is eighteen. Love is determined and defined in *Celles qu'on prend dans ses bras* (1950): Ravier has a penchant for becoming interested in women who do not love him, in women who create no dependency through gratitude, and in women who impose no responsibilities. Mlle Andriot is barely able to explain to Christine, naïve and a little unworthy, all of Ravier's complex nature.[4]

Superficially, Ravier seems to possess the arrogance one associates with the very rich and the very powerful. Indeed, at the beginning of the play he declares that he is both rich and powerful. Elsewhere in the play, however, an atmosphere of humility, even of uncertainty, surrounds Ravier; it is particularly apparent whenever he speaks with Mlle Andriot. His position with respect to women is precarious, surely, for Mlle Andriot tells Christine too much of Ravier's confessions. Mlle Andriot, whether old friend and hearer of confessions, or something more than that, suffers the malady of women scorned: attracted to Ravier for many years, she is unwilling to witness an affair between Ravier and Christine. Scorned, she becomes dangerous to Ravier for, as the title of the play suggests, she is not one of those women he has taken into his arms.

At the conclusion of the play Christine seeks Ravier's help on behalf of her father. In doing so, she automatically places herself in a position of being grateful to Ravier and thus risks her own defeat. Gratitude is a killer of love in Montherlantian psychology. In a curious reversal, however, Ravier at first dismisses her and then accepts her back, especially after he convinces himself that Christine does not love him. Still, she becomes false in his eyes because she poses a possible threat to his freedom. While he accepts Christine finally, despite evidence of her "lesser" qualities, Ravier anticipates that his affair with her will make him suffer.

Celles qu'on prend dans ses bras, while having an intelligible definition of its own, can best be understood as a link to *Les Jeunes Filles.* Costals, of course, is continually concerned about the "baggage" of life, he is constantly afraid that women will impose their sentimentality—in the form of love or gratitude, for example—in an unconscious way, but in a way that may somehow diminish him. The play at first seems a game of paradoxes, for Ravier's ideas of love are unusual, and the paradoxes tend to baffle audiences looking for some meaningful concept of love. Ravier defends himself with his *dominio;* his anticipation of suffering arises from his awareness that a portion of his freedom is sacrificed to a portion of his sensuality. He is depicted as larger than life, but he is a monster in a monstrous world of erratic emotionalism. He is the opposite of Giraudoux's Apollon de Bellac, who sees beauty where it is least visible. For Ravier, beauty in all senses is little more than a piece of art in his private collection, an object to be admired in a detached way. Christine, too, is an object of the art collection: she is a spiritually diminished human, standing well below Ravier's towering egotism of uncertain charm. But we are concerned with Montherlantian studies of humans, and it must be admitted that his Ravier is drawn with disconcerting truth.

VII Brocéliande

Montherlant's *Brocéliande* (1956) is remarkably dissimilar to his other theatrical works; it follows a unique pattern *sui generis* that may at first dismay and confuse audiences. In one way, the author obfuscates understanding of this work by emphasizing, in his prefatory notes, that *Brocéliande* is a sad play in an envelope of half-gaiety.[5] Hence it seems to be a tragedy with humor, at least as the playwright describes it. Moreover, Montherlant underlines the unmistakable importance of suicide in the play, or at least he indicates his intention to study one aspect of the nature of suicide. Of course, there is nothing new in finding tragedy in comedy—as nineteenth-century critics discovered—but some critics forgot, in their passion for antithesis and paradox, that all major comedic phenomena do spring from tragic circumstances of varying importance and varying degree. Outwardly, comedy's purpose is to make us laugh and, despite implications of the tragic, the final curtain should add sense to the comedy's definition, bringing us to a feeling of completion. Montherlant's "envelope of half-gaiety" that shrouds his sad play, however, is nothing more than a shift of emphasis familiar in twentieth-century theater; it is a technique used by Ionesco, for example.

Until the last two scenes of Act III, Montherlant dutifully adheres to what can be described as a traditional form of comedy. M. Persilès, at the age of fifty-nine, and his wife lead a comfortable bourgeois existence in Paris. His life is devoid of grandeur or quality; it possesses an apparent contentment of limited scope but has grown more arid with the passing years. M. Persilès is something of a mindless creature at the beginning of the play. But he emerges from the negative atmosphere of his milieu to become suddenly aware of a new self-importance and a new dignity. M. Edgar Bonnet de la Bonnetière serves as the catalyst.

The gentleman with the odd name is a librarian at the Institut de Numismatique. He arrives to inform M. Persilès that through the illegitimate line M. Persilès is a descendant of Saint Louis. The comedic force of the play is thus set in motion, for descent from Saint Louis, in France, has the same ring of absurdity as descent from John of Gaunt or William the Conqueror. Like Monsieur Jourdain in Molière's *Le Bourgeois Gentilhomme*, whose life is enriched when he discovers that he has been speaking prose all along, M. Persilès abruptly finds his world enlarged and infinitely filled with possibility. The revelation that leads to his new grandeur comes to him as if in a dream, and it comes from the dream world of Brocéliande—traditionally the forest home of Merlin. His world becomes fianlly more enchantment than dream.

La Bonnetière is an unworldly emissary, and Montherlant emphasizes his mystical quality by first describing him in the *dramatis personae* as forty-eight years old but "ageless." By analogy the Institut de Numismatique becomes in itself a sort of magic forest because it has the power of producing grandeur. M. Persilès' reaction to La Bonnetière's news is cautious, however, for he cannot entirely savor the full meaning of his lineage. His world becomes a dream world of grandeur, of heraldry, of nobility, but all seen through the eyes of a bourgeois. He is also furious that knowledge of his link to glory was not revealed to him in his youth, at an age when heraldry gives to youth, according to M. Persilès, the mystery of grandeur; he regrets that he did not then have the nobiliary *de* before his name, for it could have erased his callowness.

Despite his preliminary caution and his regret that the news has reached him late in life, he does gradually become a new man. M. Persilès becomes a man of letters, devoting himself assiduously to extensive research on the life and times of Saint Louis; he writes articles on the subject, although they are for the most part plagiarisms of works he reads. The metamorphosis becomes more serious: he kneels before an employee from the gas company as a humble gesture of mercy—precisely because Saint Louis knelt when he washed the feet of the poor. His tone of speech, according to Mme Persilès, becomes disturbingly "royal." In his new world he begins to concern himself with France's fate: he tries to withdraw from his milieu, which he claims to represent insipid mediocrity. As he withdraws, he no longer is able to communicate with Mme Persilès, and his wife implores La Bonnetière to uncover some valid link between her and a noble past that would permit her to live on a level with her husband. She also pleads with her husband to understand his manhood as a vital force not in need of the magic of Brocéliande. Too late, her efforts do little more than push M. Persilès further into his enchanted world.

Montherlant's technique of dramatic conclusion is curiously employed in *Brocéliande*. Until the very end of the play, less one scene, the play is a comedy. Speaking out of context, Mme Persilès proposes a farewell drink for La Bonnetière, and she claims that the play ought to end happily.[6] Were the play to end at this point, it could be described as a comedy of the absurd. Like Molière's principal characters at the conclusions of his plays, M. Persilès would remain unchanged, and his ludicrous posture would remain fixed. But Montherlant is not content to abandon his play so quickly or to leave it in a traditional form. He adds a final scene portraying M. Persilès' suicide and thereby violently imposes tragedy on comedy.[7] The scene is really an afterstatement, for the audience does not follow M. Persilès to his death by way of dialogue; it hears only the sound of the gun.

I consider *Brocéliande,* but without its final scene, the only comedy of merit that he has created. The gaiety of the play is superbly drawn by Montherlant, and it suggests but does not imitate Molière's technique. Certainly the technique of repetition appears with good effect. Mme Persilès repeats that she must play the piano whenever her husband exasperates her; the maid, Emilie, repeats that M. Persilès smokes too much. Insanity—on both the comic and the tragic levels—is an important part of the play: the discussion of heraldry, for example, as spoken by La Bonnetière, has a quality of madness about it. It may be only a sample of wry humor, however, for madness in Montherlant's works often speaks logic. Montherlant demonstrates that he can use surprise to good effect, and the final moments of the play are filled with surprises. He also is familiar with *lazzi* for comedic effect. Of course, *l'absurde* stamps the play throughout. He is even capable of laughing at himself in the rare moment when M. Persilès regrets his descent from Saint Louis through a female line.[8]

Balanced with the comedy, of course, is the disturbing tragedy of M. Persilès' suicide. It is unjust to note that his act has no prior motivation: if madness pervades the drama, it is a madness that ultimately explains M. Persilès' death. In retrospect, he ceases to be mad on the comic level. His is a genuine insanity that lives and thrives in a comic situation that hides his sickness. When Mr. Persilès is finally shaken from his enchantment, he says few words that show his defeat, but they are enough. He must again think of himself as a commoner, a *roturier,* and for the old man the change back is too swift. Like Léon of *Les Célibataires,* he seeks sleep, a symbol of his wish to die, and sleep becomes the only way to endure a meaningless existence. He claims he feels like Don Quixote when he stopped being mad.[9]

I find *Brocéliande* the most intriguing of the plays treated in this chapter. First, Montherlant's ability to create original theater is clearly demonstrated by the play; second, Montherlant shows that he is keenly aware, especially in his mature works, of the invisible machinations capable of driving man to greatness or to destruction, and *Brocéliande* is a fine example of his awareness. Finally, his addition of the suicide scene at the end of the play is a brilliant coup de théâtre that lends depth to M. Persilès' character. Yet we find in all of the plays of contemporary theme the seed of Montherlant's major dramas.

CHAPTER 5

The Culmination: The Great Plays

I *Montherlant's Disciplined Focus*

THE plays of contemporary theme, by comparison with Montherlant's major dramatic works studied in the present chapter, are the playwright's finger exercises. Montherlant's superb dramatic orchestrations, ranging from *La Reine morte,* first produced in 1942, to *La Guerre civile,* produced in 1965, display a wide range of subject matter, of period, and of milieu. Only *Port-Royal,* which sets in relief a historical episode relating to seventeenth-century Jansenism, may properly be termed a French play about France. But if there is an apparent variety of subject matter, period, and milieu in the major works, it should be examined with care, for Montherlant is still concerned with his mystique and with his universal man as proclaimed in "Syncrétisme et alternance." Rome is at the heart of the mystique, of course, a Rome that perhaps never existed. By analogy, by extension, Renaissance Spain serves to continue the mystique of Rome; again by analogy, Portugal, at least in *La Reine morte,* belongs to the Roman lineage; Renaissance Italy, too, emerges from the identical mystique. All of the plays fit into the pattern of past grandeur, although it is striking that his latest play, *La Guerre civile,* is the only one that treats a genuine Roman theme. Yet the "Roman theme" is not precisely the heart of the play, for *La Guerre civile,* as its title indicates, is concerned with the general theme of civil war; moreover, its scenes are not in Rome but on foreign battlegrounds. If *La Reine morte* is laid in legendary Portugal, *Le Maître de Santiago* and *Le Cardinal d'Espagne* have the aura but not the acute focus of Spain. *Don Juan* also belongs to the "Spanish cycle," but its many eccentricities remove it from the mainstream of Montherlant's dramatic progression. Finally, Renaissance Italy breathes again in *Malatesta*—although hero and situation could be made Spanish by a simple transformation.

In the major plays we are also concerned with the tragic hero, although not with an unshaded hero always towering over his tragic situation. Contrary to popular belief, Montherlant's heroes are less than all-powerful, less than adamantly convinced of their rightness, and less than supremely endowed with absolute perfection. It is precisely their lack of perfection that permits us to see them as entirely human. They are multifaceted creatures capable of a multiplicity of acts that are sometimes irrational; theirs is a human psychology that Montherlant claims as entirely normal. They are syncretic beings constantly alternating their poles: when we think we have at last seized the sense of one of his heroes we are likely to see the same hero transformed into something different. We are nevertheless looking at the same hero in the same set of circumstances. He is not new or changed; he is very much the same individual. The syncretic concept has already been revealed in Montherlant's novels, of course. Costals of *Les Jeunes Filles* is such a multifaceted hero (or non-hero) who displays in the four novels a gamut of traits that in essence explain the "whole man" he is intended to represent. In the novel, however, Montherlant is never aware of artistic limitations, or so it would seem. In the theater he is bound by the limitations of traditional theater to explicate his hero briefly and succinctly. Since he demonstrates, with rare exceptions, that he is capable of managing a disciplined art form without losing sight of his poetic language, his theater emerges as his primary contribution to letters.

II La Reine morte (Queen after Death)

The second (published) version of *La Reine morte* (1942), requested by Jean-Louis Vaudoyer of the Comédie Française, has undergone a vast array of interpretations, and I do not wish to exclude by any means the author's own extensive notes.[1] Since the play was written and performed during the German occupation, it is sometimes seen as a link to France's upheaval at that moment of history; others have preferred to acknowledge Montherlant's own interpretations of the play; and between the two poles there exists a mass of interpretation that has found unusual, and often original, values in the work. Despite the author's sincerity in wishing to explicate his play to his audiences, and especially to a body of unyielding and often hostile critics—for anti-Montherlantianism is a popular pastime in France—it is probable that the sense of the play comes into focus best without the playwright's help. *La Reine morte* offers a brilliant psychological study of characters who should be examined and deciphered within the framework of the play itself. It is in no way paradoxical, of course, that an art form as understood by it creator appears as something different to others. Montherlant, always aware of the agony of creation, is also aware that a work of art must inevitably be torn from its creator, the umbilical cord must be severed, and the work must live or die in a world apart. I have left to a subsequent chapter Montherlant's curious inability to understand that his public, as well as his critics, must determine the value of his plays as they are seen and interpreted by actors, and not as they are intended from his point of view.

Purists who trace the legend of Inés de Castro to some point of historicity in the fourteenth century will fail to achieve the flavor of Montherlant's *La Reine morte*. His route vaguely begins with Camões' *Os Lusiadas*,[2] but it more clearly starts with Vélez de Guevara's *Reinar después de morir*.[3] Readers of Spanish will find a more closely parallel interpretation of the legend, especially as portrayed by Vélez de Guevara, in Alejandro Casona's *Corona de amor y muerte* (1955), a play as entirely Hispanic in flavor as Montherlant's is un-Hispanic and French. Many writers have been fascinated with the legend, but only Montherlant has created an entirely new play: his is a unique drama possessing at once the familiar stamp of Montherlantian psychology as well as the stamp of great French theater which requires an attention to *la morale*—to the psychological and moral dilemma—rather than to action *per se*. In this sense, *La Reine morte* resembles the plays of Corneille and Racine. We have only to recall that Corneille's *Le Cid*, despite its close source in Spanish drama, is a French play about Frenchmen because of its insistence upon *la morale* as understood in the first half of the seventeenth century. There is a touch of the Cornelian in *La Reine morte*, although in such a definition one risks findings parallels that are coincidental. Montherlant's play is a study of duty—the Cornelian *devoir*—in counterbalance with the passions; but King Ferrante's passions, and not his duty, prevail in *La Reine morte*.

Ferrante of Portugal, following the normal dictates of political necessity and the persuasions of his own aging, arranges a marriage of convenience between his son Pedro and the Infanta of Navarre. His arrangements, nevertheless, are blocked by circumstances beyond his control. First, Pedro and Inés de Castro have already been secretly married in a religious ceremony, and Inés is expecting a child; second, Ferrante, aware of the Pope's hostility, knows that the marriage will not be annulled by the Church; and finally, the enemy from Africa—an episode that immediately recalls *Le Cid*—has inflicted damage on the Portuguese state. Of course, Ferrante's knowledge of these catastrophes is learned gradually, for the play's exposition poses only the immediate problem of Pedro's unwillingness to marry the Infanta. In this respect, the play stands apart from the classic French tragedies in which the entire dilemma is made explicit in the exposition. The opening scenes of *La Reine morte* do not contain all of the pieces of the drama: Ferrante's tragedy grows as the play progresses, and we realize the possibilities of tragedy only as he, Ferrante, reacts to each obstacle. It is a play that suggests a tapestry of frustrations whose threads are always linked to Ferrante.

Ferrante is the only character that fixes our attention in *La Reine morte*. He appears to be larger than life because the world as he envisions it holds a grandeur and an idealism beyond human understanding. At first sight Ferrante risks being seen as something larger than the Aristotelian hero, hence too unreal to be absorbed by the audience's understanding and sympathy. But this first vision of Ferrante is soon replaced by another: he is simply a human who, by contrast with others, looms over them. His sense of duty, for example, is a major motivating force: duty to state and duty to himself, even duty to others who surround him. Despite his enormous dignity, despite the nobility of his language and manner, he finally appears as entirely human. His eventual fall, because it is a fall from a lofty pedestal to the depths of defeat, strikes one as exceptionally long and agonizing, however; again its length is measured as a contrast, for others have their feet more firmly planted on the ground. Ferrante is a human bathed in anger because the inadequacies of his fellow humans frustrate him. It is clear at the play's beginning that his son Pedro is a personification of mediocrity. It soon becomes clear that his court counselors, Egas Coelho and Alvar Gonçalvès, both involved in complicated webs of intrigue, are untrustworthy and treacherous. Surprisingly, at least in a Montherlantian work, Ferrante is most sympathetic to the women. He at first favors Inés de Castro, perhaps because she does not impose herself consciously in the face of Ferrante's will. Again, he is entirely sympathetic toward the Infanta of Navarre, for he is able to reciprocate the angry frustrations of this masculinized woman who thinks like a statesman rather than like a woman rejected in love. Yet Ferrante reserves for himself the weight of his severest criticism, for he is totally aware of his own weaknesses, of his capacity for erring, of his innate ability to destroy others. In a large sense, his human qualities—changed into enormous defects—guarantee his own destruction: checked in every move he makes to resolve his problems, whether political or personal, he must and does act to preserve his life—and then to preserve the state. Montherlant changes Ferrante so that his "passions," or his concern for self, far outweigh his concern for Portugal; in this respect, Ferrante is not Cornelian. When Ferrante orders Inés de Casto killed, he is completely involved with the self.

I have already pointed out that *La Reine morte* is a mirror-image drama, wherein most of the characters repeat in some way the central figure, King Ferrante.[4] It is a phenomenon that makes Montherlant's play far more unique than one might expect. The mind of the Infanta is always raised to a virile level and she is totally devoid of sentimentality: her thoughts are expressed with the same tonality and the same sense of logic as those of Ferrante. Pedro is portrayed as having had in early youth the grandeur of Ferrante, or at least a tendency toward his father's grandeur; an older Pedro, as he appears in the play, is mediocre; but he reflects his father's instability, an instability that permits us to grasp the meaning of Ferrante's essential humanity. Inés de Castro, although a less carefully drawn dramatic character, gradually becomes aware of her danger and of her tragic position, especially as Ferrante pours out to her his confession of personal weakness. The correspondence of their natures, especially at the moment of Ferrante's confessions, becomes clear. The two counselors, Egas Coelho and Alvar Gonçalvès, entirely devious and egotistical, reflect Ferrante's Machiavellian nature, although their influence on Ferrante scarcely determines dramatic action. Finally, the court page Dino del Moro mirrors on the one hand Ferrante's capacity for humor—a mild humor at best— and on the other hand the human penchant for treasonous acts. Both humor and treason are implied as portions of Ferrante's nature. Of course, Ferrante is not depicted as a man possessed of a single set of character traits, for the Montherlantian hero displays the gamut of human traits, both good and bad, that the human animal has by nature: he can be "charitable," sympathetic, and generous at the same time that he is self-centered, cruel, and murderous. He can destroy others as well as kill himself. For Montherlant such a hero is the only one capable of reflecting the natural complexities of man's character. Ferrante's high pedestal is a weak structure and is more often seen as a symbol of grandeur than as grandeur itself.

Montherlant's tragedy stands apart from traditional tragedy in other ways. I have already pointed out that *La Reine morte*'s exposition does not entirely clarify the drama. It does, however, set forth at least a portion of Ferrante's dilemma. Later, the Infanta, instead of brooding over her defeat and returning immediately to Navarre, decides to remain a while longer; curiously, she tries to persuade Inés de Castro to accompany her to Spain, to join her court and be free of a political danger she foresees as inevitable. Out of sentimentality Inés chooses to remain: she loves Pedro and is about to give birth to their child. In Montherlantian terms, her sentimentality, which may strike most as entirely normal, is at the root of her weakness: Inés is feminine, therefore sentimental and therefore weak. By the same token, Pedro, both before and during his imprisonment, demonstrates clearly the nature of his mediocrity: he is pusillanimous, without will or energy to defend Inés and himself, and he is incapable of making judgments. His mediocrity is always in balance with Inés' sentimentality, and their weaknesses are displayed almost without shading. Nuance of character delineation, in fact, is remarkably absent in *La Reine morte;* only Ferrante changes, or seems to change, and the focus is riveted upon him alone.

In critical circles there is still some debate concerning Ferrante's "solution" of his problem by having Inés put to death. Some have referred to his decision as something resembling an *acte gratuit*—an act without motivation.[5] Such a view is understandable in one sense, for there seems to be little transition between Ferrante's dilemma and his decision. Yet there are many motivating forces that push Ferrante toward a need to destroy Inés. The essential force, however, derives from his *dominio,* or his basic urge to dominate, to prevail, to impose the self, whether over other humans or over obstacles. In *La Reine morte* Ferrante's domination is over himself. His tragic act is essentially a defiance of non-action, a battle against frustrations, and a last stand before the debility of old age. His concern for duty—for the strengthening of Portugal—scarcely has anything to do with his dilemma or with his solution. Ferrante's concern is primarily with himself. Completely checked from making a move, at the mercy of what he considers the slovenly human condition, he simply changes himself from a moral man into an amoral man, he sheds sympathy and charity and cloaks himself in bestiality, and in so doing he convinces himself that he reaches a genuine freedom which, in Montherlant's lexicon, is the essence of authentic manhood. If dramatic transition seems absent from the play, its absence is of superficial importance, provided a Montherlantian psychology is understood. Besides, we have already seen in the novels, especially in *Les Jeunes Filles,* that transitions from dilemma to act are not necessary: the human, whether a Costals or a Ferrante, moves insistently and even automatically to destroy any obstacle that threatens *dominio.* At the heart of Ferrante's grandeur is his amorality, but we, the audience, suggest the term; Montherlant does not.

Like Costals and Léon de Coantré, Ferrante is deeply involved in a movement toward self-destruction. Since we are concerned with tragedy, we might anticipate Ferrante's suicide or at least immolation at the hands of others. But Ferrante dies a natural death. The author's notes imply that Ferrante, becoming more than human, larger than life, as the play progresses, may possibly have been struck down by a supernatural force of unstated origin. As he is portrayed on the stage, however, Ferrante never ceases to be human—despite that awkward pedestal—and hence he cannot logically meet a death of such extraordinary origin. We find only that Inés' death is tragic. But the play is not a tragedy in the usual sense, and Ferrante, not Inés, is at the center of attention. Ferrante's death then appears more as a theatrical device created by Montherlant to serve his unique purposes: in a sense, his death is an example of the *deus ex machina* technique devised to divert dramatic focus. *La Reine morte* is really a study of treason in Montherlant's view: treason explains Pedro's mediocrity, it is Inés' sentimentality, the counselors' selfish interests, and at the play's conclusion, it is even Dino del Moro's inherent weakness.

Despite the excellent dramatic effect of the play's conclusion, the final scene comes as too abrupt a solution and is perhaps too facilely conceived; Montherlant's own explanations of Ferrante's death are not always convincing. Despite that single flaw, *La Reine morte* is a superb vehicle for Montherlantian psychology and for his *morale;* it is excellent proof of Montherlant's ability to come to terms with his multifaceted hero within a highly disciplined literary form. The tone of the drama, especially its language, recalls some of the great plays of the seventeenth century. Although *La*

Reine morte is a prose work, its rhythms often suggest a prose poem. Montherlant's richness of language rarely becomes an exaggeration of language and is always in balance with the simplicity of décor that the play requires.

III Malatesta

Ferrante in *La Reine morte* serves as one example of the multifaceted universal man described in "Syncrétisme et alternance." The best example of such a human, however, is Sigismond Malatesta of Rimini, the hero of *Malatesta* (1946).[6] Ferrante had been placed in the setting of Portugal, although the locale has nothing to do with the drama. Malatesta's Renaissance Italy, however, is a more suitable setting for Montherlant's "universal man." Malatesta is a sensitive humanist, a loyal statesman, and a devoted husband and father. He possesses a natural intelligence devoid of the intellectual; at the same time he is a sensualist rather devoid of the rational. Characteristically, Malatesta is also at times less than a humanist, disloyal when necessary, morally unrestricted, a man capable of murder or of waging war for the love of war. He is a typical Montherlantian hero displaying a vast array of apparently conflicting inner drives that make him appear both as civilized man and as animal. Of course, the transitional quality of the Renaissance may explain Malatesta's instability, but it is more to the point to note that Malatesta is not unstable in Montherlant's view: he displays as hero the enormous possibility of the human mind.

Malatesta is a tragedy, but its tragic sense stems not so much from Malatesta's death at the end of the play, or from his moral defeat after struggles with his fate, but rather from the fact that he, like Ferrante, meets obstacles that stand in the way of his freedom. Malatesta's death may be seen as a release from struggle rather than as a defeat. His freedom is blocked by Pope Paul II, who wishes to remove Malatesta from Rimini and give him instead other Italian territories to govern; Pope Paul is also disquieted by the presence in Rimini of Venetian forces. Act I offers a clear study of Malatesta as ruler of Rimini. He is determined to have vengeance on the Pope, makes his plans carefully, and regrets that Porcellio's cowardice prevents his aid. Alone, Malatesta plots the Pope's assassination, and he assumes that he will be killed by the Papal guards. Act II, which takes place in Rome, is essentially a duel of minds between Pope Paul and Malatesta. Act III is a portrayal of Malatesta in isolation, for the Pope has placed him under close watch. Malatesta's wife Isotta, free to act on his behalf, pleads successfully with the Pope to grant her husband a period of leave in Rimini. The final act is the revelation of Porcellio's treason and the murder of Malatesta. Indeed, Act IV is an entirely bizarre portion of the drama because it has almost the form of a spoken essay devoted to the universal man as Montherlant understands him. Porcellio's poisoning of Malatesta might well have concluded Act III, and the play as well; the final act stands as a lengthy footnote to the preceding portions of the drama as a gratuitous appendage. Its excessively long speeches detract from the dramatic vigor of the rest of the play. It is entirely possible that Malatesta's quality—especially his capacity for both good and evil—is too thinly traced in the first three acts: Montherlant seems to have created Act IV as a clarification of the hero's character.

The events of the final act are diverse. It offers a love scene between Malatesta and Vannella, age thirteen, obviously meant to display the virtuosity of the hero and to serve as contrast—or is it comparison?—with Malatesta's love for his wife Isotta. Again, the dialogue between Basinio and Porcellio—both men of letters attached to Malatesta's court—clearly demonstrates, although rather late in the play, that Porcellio is a mirror-image of Malatesta; hence, Montherlant repeats an effect already visible in *La Reine morte*. Even more curiously, only in the final act is the motivation for Porcellio's treason explained: Porcellio is obligated to Malatesta because the latter has saved his life.

We must again return to Montherlantian psychology, of course, which maintains that gratitude fosters obligation; since obligation prevents personal freedom, Porcellio seeks his freedom by killing Malatesta. Yet this sort of motivation is disconnected from all that takes place in the first three acts; one might at least expect that political motivation play some rôle in the murder. Montherlant constructs a play whose outcome is barely suggested until the final act, an act which he uses as his vehicle for fully describing the nature of his hero. I cannot say that his construction is weak, for Montherlant writes plays as he chooses; it is an original construction, however, and one that deserves some analysis.

The fall of Malatesta constantly dominates attention. He seems to cry out for self-destruction as a portion of personal fulfillment. First, in presenting himself before Pope Paul, who understands

Malatesta's intentions, he defies death. But the Pope is not quite ready to see Malatesta's immediate defeat: he admires Malatesta's mind, his motivations, and his nobility. The Pope and Malatesta balance each other in their appreciation of dignity and grandeur. Of course, Pope Paul is seen less as Christ's Vicar than as a man of politics. Both men display the varied aspects of Montherlant's universal man. Pope Paul's decision to curtail Malatesta's freedom is based less on a wish to elicit loyalty or thanks from Malatesta—for such a gesture would diminish Paul's stature and Malatesta's—than on a desire to preserve an equal.

The very human Pope Paul and his attendant cardinals are dramatic, highly colored foils. Certainly, the Catholic Church is totally absent from the play except when Christianity is suggested, but never meaningfully, by the occasional rote mouthings of the Pope. Montherlant treats the Church in an age when the Pope was a political force concerned with territorial expansions, with armies and with intrigues; the Church had little time to contemplate, so it would seem, the question of Christian morality. Montherlant's depiction of Pope Paul, as a sort of duplicate of Malatesta, is soundly conceived, even if it is off-center as to factual detail. He does catch the spirit of the Renaissance: the rich panoply of the Church cannot hide Paul as a man of the Renaissance destined by his fate to wear vestments. He speaks as half-man and half-Pope, although the Papal portion is merely habit. Given the fact that Malatesta and Pope Paul are really two visions of man, it is pointless to look for Christianity, morality, or dogma as motivating forces bringing about Malatesta's downfall: the closer one is to the Pope and the cardinals the farther one is from Christianity.

Malatesta is not an anti-religious play or even a drama of religious protest, nor is it a work devoted to anticlericalism. Montherlant consistently draws our attention to the man, whether prince or Pope, and to the reality of the man: his capacity for good and his capacity for evil. Supremely civilized and voraciously animalistic at the same time, Malatesta only occasionally, and then only by accident, touches the fringes of Christian morality. In a sense, Montherlant's hero recalls the poles of *spleen* and *idéal* of Baudelaire's *Les Fleurs du mal,* although Baudelaire lacks one essential ingredient of Malatesta's nature: the ability to find limitless pleasure anywhere and everywhere without feeling remorse. Montherlant's art, as it is revealed in *Malatesta,* lies in his unique ability to capture the mood of an age and to explain the age by focusing intently on a single character.

IV Le Maître de Santiago (The Master of Santiago)

Le Maître de Santiago (1947) is an enigmatic play whose sense largely depends on the viewer's own attitudes toward God and toward sacrifice in the name of God. Its sense also may be determined by one's attitude toward sacrifice as a way of life, a sacrifice that perhaps guarantees saintliness. To many, Montherlant's "Christian" drama may appear to be a study of fanaticism devoid of saintly qualities, the sort of fanaticism that stops far short of godliness and is, at best, a narrow reaching beyond the self. The self, in the latter instance, may only be a point in the mind's departure as well as the center of total concern. This is not a Jansenist play, surely, despite its almost morbid concern with discipline, with abnegation of life, and with spiritual isolation. Perhaps too much attention has been paid to Montherlant's Jansenism; the terms Jansenist and Pascalian, the twin terms of much recent criticism about Montherlant, lend an aura of grandeur to his works without clarifying them. What is usually meant by the words is dark introspection, a concern for man's fate in an evil world, or simply a voice that renounces the self.

Don Alvaro Dabo is a Knight of the Order of Santiago. He serves as the symbolic head of a Catholic group intent on carrying out effective missionary works in the Indies—that is, in the New World under the domination of sixteenth-century Spain. As usual, Montherlant chooses to create a plot of unexpected scope. Don Alvaro explains to his brethren of the Order, with strangely fanatic violence, that Spain and its overseas glories represent rottenness of the worst sort. Instead of deciding to spend a brief time in the Americas in order to help the Indians, who are subjected to the brutality of the conquistadores, Don Alvaro expresses a wish to isolate himself from all worldly commerce and concerns, to withdraw into a carefully planned isolation for the sake of contemplation, and to gain salvation. His seemingly nihilistic decision recalls for a brief moment Ferrante of *La Reine morte*, especially when the latter is most deeply concerned with both throne and soul. Don Alvaro is consistently and continuously drawn to the symbol of his Order, a white silk cape ornamented with a red sword whose hilt is in the form of a fleur-de-lys.

The first act clearly indicates the direction of the play's dramatic emphasis. Don Alvaro, so it would seem, is drawn to the external and temporal significance of his Order. By contrast, God is all but forgotten. The world has become too much for him, he does not understand it, and he ceases to want to understand it. Certainly, in rejecting missionary work in the Indies, he rejects a worldly saintliness and prefers the more direct route to salvation through a total renunciation of all temporal things. God and Christianity have no meaning whatsoever, on close examination, in terms of his salvation.

Don Alvaro is clearly a non-hero moving in a self-imposed nihilism. Yet, he controls the Order's affairs—much as Ferrante controls his affairs of state. He sends Don Enrique de Letamendi to the New World to perform missionary duties, but he carefully refrains from bestowing on him his sympathy or his kindness. Don Alvaro, possessing typically Montherlantian traits, recoils at Don Enrique's youth, a sign of mediocrity: the young man is prejudged as lacking in fineness and fitness, probably incapable of anything but failure. According to Don Alvaro, only the elderly, because their adventures are "interior" rather than born of action, are capable of genuine intelligence. Here, of course, we encounter a battle of generations already familiar in Montherlant's works. The playwright also introduces a father-daughter relationship similar to that of *Le Chaos et la nuit.* Mariana is depicted as an obstacle forever standing between her father and God. Her father has no interest in guaranteeing Mariana's happiness by permitting her marriage to the young Jacinto; his interest lies elsewhere, outside of the family sphere. Don Alvaro detests all human attachments as obstacles to grandeur—like Costals, who also seeks isolation. Mariana's father claims, for example, that it is degrading to live with a human being—he is thinking precisely of Mariana—so alien to his goal of noble proportions; surprisingly, he feels that he must "charitably" demonstrate some form of interest in human beings, knowing full well that his gestures would be empty.

Verisimilitude of character, with respect to the non-hero Don Alvaro, becomes increasingly threatened by such fanaticism. It is even more threatened when Don Bernal, of the same Order, proposes that Don Alvaro spend some time in the New World, if only to obtain a proper dowry for his daughter's wedding. The father's refusal is to be expected, of course. I am concerned that Don Bernal accuses him of taking refuge in charity—a term Montherlant repeats often in his work and often without meaning.

At this point the play moves far indeed from God and godliness and becomes a suspension of holiness. Don Alvaro's prosaic struggle is with his temporal imperfections and is far less a combat to preserve his soul. There is verisimilitude in the portrait of Don Alvaro as long as the weaknesses of the man and of the father remain in the foreground of attention. Don Bernal is entirely perceptive when he accuses Don Alvaro of permitting his romantic sense of chivalry to blind his reason. Don Alvaro is not charitable because he has left reason behind.[7] The word has no meaning as it appears in the play, and Montherlant's discussion of the term is equally baffling, for he seems to be describing an angry spitefulness; certainly it is a pejorative word as it is found in *Le Maître de Santiago.*

The institution of family, since it is an obstacle to grandeur, is condemned by Don Alvaro. But the Order, on the other hand, is a noble institution because it draws to it men who have been selected. The Order is the real family of elected spirits with common beliefs and noble concepts. It does not impose attachments, whether through love, affection, or obligations, and hence it permits access to a grandeur that the family could never have. Oddly enough, Mariana gradually comes out of the shadows imposed by her father, just as Pascualita in *Le Chaos et la nuit* emerges from Celestino's nihilism. Where she was once naïve and mediocre, she becomes now, without preface or transition, the mirror-image of Don Alvaro; Mariana suddenly possesses a masculine outlook that parallels somewhat that of the Infanta in *La Reine morte.* Through a strange metamorphosis she becomes less an obstacle standing between her father and God and more a co-conspirator of her father. She seeks a life in which courage is needed for survival. Still believing she may marry Jacinto, she tells him that children water down the relationship between husband and wife. Don Bernal is justified in comparing her with her father, although perhaps less so in adding that she is more intelligent than he. Mariana's serious statement that she does not wish to be happy prepares the way for an eventual understanding with her father.

Count Soria, come to convince Don Alvaro of the king's supposed wish that he go to the New World, a plot that originally involved Mariana, is betrayed by this newly evolved Mariana who reveals the story's falseness. Marriage with Jacinto becomes irrevocably closed to her. She is now determined to seek a level of understanding with her father and, in so doing, to renounce worldly matters. To reach this lofty level, however, she must sacrifice herself totally.

I do not find even a trace of romantic sentiment for God in the final scene of the play. It is a scene portraying the complete renunciation of life by father and daughter, both of whom are more mad than divine. What I do find is a fanaticism spewed forth from Don Alvaro's egomania; his attention is not on God but rather on the marvelous adventure of getting there. It is an adventure far more attractive than a journey to the Indies, and it is one that a young man, such as Letamendi, could never undertake or appreciate. Don Alvaro displays less the nobility of a saintly Order than the viciousness of Satan, for in the name of God he is willing to see the destruction of Spain and even of the Universe, provided the destruction becomes a means of achieving his salvation. The final scene returns to the symbolism of the Order's cape, which hangs on the wall throughout the play. The father uses the cape to cover both his shoulders and his daughter's in a gesture meant to underscore their ecstasy and their oblivion—or else their madness and their surrender of life.

If my remarks have stressed the non-Christian elements of *Le Maître de Santiago,* they should not by any means persuade the reader that Montherlant ignores Catholicism in the strange portrayal of Don Alvaro. The author is aware that his work contains both a pagan and a Christian scope.[8] Montherlant attempts to explain his non-hero's Christianity, but he sees Don Alvaro as a Christian misunderstood by the modern public. Of course, Don Alvaro recalls the asceticism of an older Church, or the complete renunciation of the world by those who seek salvation in this life. Unfortunately, Montherlant's character, while ascetic enough, is too remote from the Christian idealism proposed by his Church; his views of marriage, of the family, and of his daughter, for example, are remote from Christian morality. One wonders at his salvation as one wonders how his fanaticism, replacing Christian morality, can ever soar heavenward. One wonders, finally, if he has a soul. By the same token, Mariana emerges as a replica of her father. Her metamorphosis from innocence to fanaticism is too sudden, too poorly defined dramatically, to convince us of her credibility: her womanhood seems a descent into madness. Of course, one may always indulge in a Freudian interpretation, but I find such an interpretation too facile. Is Montherlant somehow at the edge of a Jansenist portrayal of Don Alvaro and Mariana?

As I have already indicated, the play lacks the Christianity of Jansenism; only the flavor of asceticism suggests Jansenism. Whether or not *Le Maître de Santiago* is a Christian, or Catholic, play is perhaps beside the point. It is a superb study of man's mind in chaos and even of man's capacity to inflict chaos on others. God is in the play only through an external symbolism—the cape of the Order, for example—and the drama is Christian only if the spectator wills it. Entirely enigmatic, the play is understood by way of individual conscience; for that reason there will always be multiple interpretations of *Le Maître de Santiago*.

V Port-Royal

After *Malatesta* and *Le Maître de Santiago,* one wonders if Montherlant's *Port-Royal* (1954), devoted with great care to a historical-religious moment of seventeenth-century France, can be a genuinely Christian play. As usual, the playwright anticipates critical comment and exposes in great detail his creative *modus operandi* in a concise preface helpful to those who appreciate the quality of his historical approach.[9] He is heavily indebted to Sainte-Beuve's nineteenth-century account of Port-Royal, although Sainte-Beuve is not Montherlant's single source: Montherlant has examined correspondence relating to the dissolution of Jansenist Port-Royal, and he was already familiar with the works of Pascal, defender of Jansenism in his *Lettres provinciales.* Montherlant's major contribution to the still fascinating story of the Catholic heresy of Jansenism is his ability to bring dramatic focus on the events of a few hours, and to restrict his focus to a three-act drama. Because of his close attention to historicity—he does admit to a few changes and he indicates what they are—and especially because of his poetic accuracy in portraying the atmosphere of Jansenism's tragedy, he should rank with Sainte-Beuve. He has caught in his brief work all of the frustration, the desperation, the sense of utter isolation, as well as the vast capacity for faith, of the sisters in the Port-Royal convent in Paris. He manages this sensitive undertaking by treating but a single day in August, 1664.

Port-Royal to my mind is Montherlant's single "Catholic" drama, although the play is not an argument for Jansenism. His other plays to which he ascribes the term "Catholic"—*Le Maître de Santiago* and even, according to Montherlant, *La Ville dont le prince est un enfant*—are Catholic in a negative sense. I have already underlined the nihilism of the first play, *Le Maître de San-*

tiago; the two boys of *La Ville* are temporarily defeated by the perversion of Catholicism. Yet Catholicism *per se* is scarcely at the heart of the plays, despite Montherlant's view. Of course, the imaginative spectator may, if he wishes, take one more intellectual stride after the final curtain and insist upon Catholicism, or even Jansenism, in the plays, although such a stride must be based upon speculation. In *Port-Royal* the sisters' Christianity is understood as always present and always clear.

Certainly, the sisters of Port-Royal are portrayed as entirely human; they have a humanity that Don Alvaro never possesses. Attention is drawn almost at once to Sister Angélique de Saint-Jean, to her rigidity that seems unchanging at first, but which slowly evaporates into doubt at the conclusion of the play. Treason, too, moves through the convent: the treason of Sister Flavie can only be examined in terms of natural human weakness, for she lacks the quality of Sister Angélique, whose loyalty to the convent is assured both by her rigorous training and by her rank as niece of Arnauld. Moreover, the whole tenor of the dialogue among the sisters is at once strikingly worldly and unworldly at the same time. Montherlant peoples the convent with figures now become familiar: the sisters explain their doubts, show that their faith is not flawless, and that they are women, after all. Their humanity creates a bizarre tension of its own in the play: the world must be shut out, but there seems to be no way to do so. Worldly *dominio* poses a constant threat to their humanity.

Worldly *dominio* is symbolized by the Archbishop de Péréfixe, who orders that all religious persons sign the official *formulaire* of obedience to the Church of Rome—and coincidentally to Louis XIV. Montherlant carries the symbolism a step further, at least in his stage directions, by twice referring to the Archbishop and his accompanying throng of courtiers as a group of colorful, monstrous insects bent upon destruction. Within the play itself, Montherlant creates a parallel symbol of a mysterious Beast in conflict with the Holy Spirit. It is a struggle that occurs in Sister Marie-Claire's dream which she relates to Sister Gabrielle. In Sister Marie-Claire's dream the Beast speeds between the Louvre—the Royal Palace—and Port-Royal, all the while roaring its frightening power. Sister Gabrielle understands the dream as a summary of the history of Port-Royal: it is the story of constant struggle between evil and good and between the temporal and the spiritual. Of course, the symbolism, once taken out of the play's context, immediately recalls Montherlant's concern with man's movement between primitivism and divinity. In *Port-Royal* the sisters are determined to resist the Beast. Later in the play, the symbolism is repeated, but this time in the context of Mother Angélique's comment that while Port-Royal may kill the Beast—for Port-Royal can impose its own *dominio* of faith—the Beast will ultimately kill Port-Royal, for Péréfixe's temporal power is the stronger.

I am sure that Montherlant proceeds from this symbolism to the dramatic sense of the play. What destroys the convent is its determination to resist. It dares to be different, and in Montherlantian terms those who dare to be different are doomed to destruction. What man may conceive within the framework of Christian morality—Jansenism, for example—is singular and alien. The fact that Jansenism may have done scant harm is of little importance: the sisters are condemned for their singularities, despite evidence proclaiming their essential Christianity. And so man, if he is an alien standing on the edge of common understanding, is condemned on earth for being different, and he is isolated and doomed while he is still alive. The symbolism of the Beast—or bestiality—simply recalls man's complexities. Péréfixe is a beast devoid of Christianity, and he may be compared with Pope Paul of *Malatesta* or with Don Alvaro of *Le Maître de Santiago*. The Archbishop is close to Montherlant's universal man—but so is Sister Flavie, who betrays her convent. Of course, Montherlant employs symbolism at yet another level in *Port-Royal,* although largely for dramatic effect: twelve sisters leave Port-Royal and are replaced by twelve sisters. As Péréfixe arrives at the convent, one hears twelve strokes of the clock. These are superficial effects related to décor, just as the cape in *Le Maître de Santiago* is related to it.

The dialogue of the play may strike many as diverse and even confusing. Port-Royal unfolds slowly from its lengthy exposition. Dialogue is perhaps too random, too little interlocking, but Montherlant has the difficult task of establishing in a brief time both the unique character and the multifaceted nature of his subjects; his task is made doubly difficult by the necessity of abiding by at least the major facts of history. If there is confusion, it results from the multiplicity of focuses, and the play deserves, for that reason, to be examined several times. Surprisingly, it is a play of great density—*dense* in the French sense of the word—because the play moves along several levels of understanding: the Catholic, the human, and the symbolic; the spectator or reader must be prepared to keep in mind these three levels of understanding to grasp fully both the sense and the atmosphere of *Port-Royal.*

Montherlant is also a master of what might be called "silent drama." *La Reine morte* has such a silent drama at its conclusion when Ferrante and Inés, both dead, lie on the stage: Dino del Moro moves from the side of the king to the newly crowned Inés in a wordless scene intended to emphasize the boy's treason. This technique, which Montherlant has developed with great skill, is repeated in *Le Maître de Santiago,* when Don Alvaro enfolds himself and his daughter in the Order's cape. In *Port-Royal,* the theatrical device is used to greatest effect. Sister Angélique's doubt about her faith ends the play, and there dialogue ceases. Afterward, the audience observes Sister Françoise's astonishment at Sister Angélique's words; it hears then the sound of None, symbolizing the death of Christ; there follows the sound of carriages passing in the streets outside the convent. A sister suddenly appears on stage and departs at once, her face showing her horror; then the audience hears singing in the chapel as the new Mother Superior arrives followed by twelve new sisters, all of whom are dressed in black. The silent drama is punctuated by two periods when the stage is empty of players. Montherlant's technique is an intensely studied one: the total black of the new sisters' garb, for example, contrasts with the cross worn on the habit of the sisters of Port-Royal. Again, the brilliant insect colors of Péréfixe's entourage contrasts with the bleakness of the convent itself.

The final mute scene also directs attention to the play's historicity, although the play's humanity is more important. The sisters are not portrayed as inhumanly pure or less sane than the world on the outside of the convent, for they display, quite to the contrary, a gamut of human qualities. More curiously, the Montherlantian women of *Port-Royal* offer excellent proof of the playwright's ability to move away from an Andrée Hacquebaut or a Solange, those feminine curiosities of *Les Jeunes Filles,* and to move toward women as they are. Of course, the sisters are not duplicates of one another, for they possess the dignity and the nobility Montherlant usually ascribes to men. I nevertheless see Montherlant's stamp of masculinity in the play, just as his stamp of masculinity is placed on the Infanta of *La Reine morte.*

VI Don Juan

The literary world, I think, is scarcely surprised to discover, especially when it views the total work of Montherlant, the curiously illusive flaw. Few creative artists of stature manage to complete their careers without giving birth to such a flaw, which always holds a special fascination. We are fascinated because the artist suddenly emerges from his creative obscurity and appears finally to be human. Of course, there is always the grave danger that the public may judge an author's literary career on the basis of a single work that stands apart from the mainstream of the career. There is an even graver danger: the author of such a curious literary "child" may spring to the defense of his work, perhaps without justification, and place in temporary doubt the quality of his other labors.

Don Juan (1958) is such a flaw in the work of Montherlant. Despite attempts by several critics to underline the solid substance, the play really lacks, and to point to a solidity of dramatic construction that it also lacks, this addition to the vast repertory of the Don Juan legend will have to be judged as a bizarre phenomenon.[10] It lies quite apart from the legend and may in time serve only as a curious footnote to it. What Montherlant attempts to create is a serious play in accordance with the legend, but he adds two elements that defeat its seriousness: first, an attempt at humor, and again, an attempt at pseudophilosophic criticism. On rare occasions Montherlant can be a humorous writer—in *Brocéliande,* for example—but his humor is usually absent; or else he is humorous on occasion but bleakly so. More often than not, he is as humorless as Celestino chasing pigeons in the park in *Le Chaos et la nuit;* although we may laugh at Celestino's ludicrous act of protest and of defeat, we also are familiar with the tragedy that inspires his act. There is perhaps a moment of humor in *Port-Royal* when Sisters Julie and Flavie demonstrate the familiar Molière technique of repetition. Generally speaking, however, humor is not Montherlant's forte, and when it occurs, it is low-keyed, often approaching the absurd; Montherlant seems self-conscious when trying to be humorous, probably because he tries too hard. If *Don Juan* is intended as a major attempt at comedy, it falls far short of its goal. It is an awkward comedy, and worse, it is often in bad taste. I sense that the playwright's humor may have been influenced by Charlie Chaplin, especially in *Don Juan,* for the play does have the flavor of the chaplinesque mixture of the absurd and the sublime. Indeed, Montherlant admits to a liking for such comedy.[11] Montherlant misunderstands to what degree the sublime can enhance tragic truth: in undertaking to write his *Don Juan* he should have avoided any absurdity without meaning. For example, he could have eliminated, at the close of the first act, the throwing of chamber pots out of windows. The sub-farcical action and dialogue of his second act, bringing to the fore the Countess and the Commander, do not lead the audience to an understanding of psychological development. Again, the innovations of the final act do not assure the sense of the drama or conclude it, especially since transitions are missing. In his notes Montherlant refers to the last act as *pathétique,* but the term falls short of its mark. After the play's first performance, when it met with a roaring disapproval from critics and public alike, Montherlant determined to explicate his play in his own way; however, his explications obfuscate rather than clarify the work.

I have noted that Montherlant's humor, supposedly chaplinesque, does not quite come off in the play. A second major element defeats the play: the playwright uses literary criticism as a portion of the play itself. It is always dangerous for a dramatist to use the public stage as a sort of Hyde Park Corner from which he can lash out against matter unrelated to the play. *Don Juan* is a forum for Montherlant, who attacks doctors, men of letters, and psychologists, all intellectuals intent on analyzing Montherlant's literary works. The playwright drags the matter of criticism into his drama in a meaningless way. His introduction of these professional men seems to stem from his wish to explain negatively what his work is—it is Don Juan's rôle to counter with an explanation of what it is not. Yet Montherlant insists that his play be examined without reference to his private life, hence to his private views. In order to grind his axe, he creates an episode involving his detractors and his critics that quickly becomes a mad mixture of Chaplin and Molière, although without the greatness of either comedian. Molière would agree, I think, that Montherlant's attempt to create a genuinely modern version of the Don Juan legend suffers from his having forgotten that the legend is always modern, and that it does not need to be brought up to date by artificial forcing. More important, he seems to have forgotten the sense of the legend.

I prefer to think of *Don Juan* as Montherlant's magnificent failure; it is magnificent because it is so remote from the usual high quality of his theater. But Molière could not write tragedy, and Montherlant cannot generally write comedy, although *Brocéliande* shows a strong capability. This play will undoubtedly be read out of curiosity by those tracing the Don Juan legend through world literature and will not often be read for amusement.

VII Le Cardinal d'Espagne

With *Le Cardinal d'Espagne* (1960) Montherlant creates a quasi-historical play whose primary importance as psychological drama far exceeds its importance as historical documentation. It is a close interpretation of the events surrounding the sixteenth century Spain of Cardinal Francisco Ximenez de Cisneros and of Juana la Loca (Jeanne la Folle). Montherlant simply follows in the footsteps of a multitude of French playwrights—it is enough to cite Corneille and Racine—who have molded history and sometimes legend to create works that are contemporary and universal studies of man. Montherlant denies that this play is historical, although he asserts the historical validity of certain of his dramatic details.[12] He is at his best whenever he tries to recreate the atmosphere and the spirit of a past age as background for his psychological studies. He is aware, of course, that drama often cannot sustain the span of true history, although *Port-Royal* might well prove the opposite, and he is also aware that historical details can encumber dramatic truths.

Despite Montherlant's interpretations of *Le Cardinal d'Espagne,* designed to direct the audience to a clear understanding of his drama, he often fails to reveal in his notes what he has actually portrayed on the stage. The playwright sees a clear parallel, for example, between Malatesta and Cisneros, quite possibly because both characters are under the influence of the Renaissance: they are multifaceted beings, to be sure. Yet it would not be correct to emphasize the parallel, for the Renaissance serves only as décor for his drama. More evident in the characters of *Le Cardinal d'Espagne* is an *aveuglement*—a blindness—that prevents their knowing what or who they really are, a blindness that symbolizes loss of identity. Despite the extensive arguments of the Montherlantian notes, his drama is better understood as a further clarification, or as an extension, of *La Reine morte.* Cisneros is an expansion of Ferrante: to be sure, he is Ferrante in Cardinal's robes, with sandals and hair shirt. And like Alvaro of *Le Maître de Santiago,*

Cisneros also has a fanaticism that has little to do with Christianity. Ferrante, too, is devoid of Christianity; more like Ferrante, Cisneros possesses a love of power coupled with a strong hatred of his fellow man. He always appears to be on the verge of soaring to spiritual heights but is caught up in earthly duties; he is in constant struggle, a spiritual struggle between union with God and entrapment in earthly mud. Where Ferrante's motivations are somewhat unclear, however, Cisneros' are entirely lucid: he wishes to stay alive and be involved in a world of action. He states that things must never be half-done; they must be done *terriblement.* His nephew Cardona further defines the sense of his life by relating that his uncle, in acting *terriblement,* wishes to ensure that he is alive. Of course, Cardona might have explained Ferrante's murder of Inés de Castro in exactly the same way; the transition from motivation to action is identical for Ferrante and for Cisneros, but the transition is clear only in *Le Cardinal d'Espagne.*

The play also enlarges on the theme of treason, a theme familiar in Montherlant's works. We have already noted the moral treason of Pedro, the implicit treason of the court and the spiritual treason of Dino in *La Reine morte,* for example. Cisneros is surrounded by treachery, but it is most evident in Cardona, his nephew, whose defection is close and therefore dangerous. Cardona's essential weakness is defined early in the play: his mediocrity, like Pedro's, guarantees treason. His supposed readiness to defend the power play of Cisneros is false. Yet, despite his treason, he is able after Cisneros' death to ask forgiveness for his crime. While Cardona's treason is of primary importance, it is nevertheless true that the treason of all men makes them enemies of Cisneros.

There exists a further link between *Le Cardinal d'Espagne* and *La Reine morte.* The masculinized Infanta of Navarre, representing the statesman's strength of will, is an early image of Juana la Loca. With Cisneros, she dominates most of the second act. External evidence of her madness is noted by Montherlant within the play, but her speeches—they are really monologues—have about them a lucidity that belies madness. In her speeches there is also the continuous tone of rebuttal so often characteristic of Montherlant's dialogue. Nonetheless, the Queen's words have a constant quality about them, for she speaks with a reality of which Cisneros is incapable. The Cardinal is astonished at her candor; he is shocked by her awareness of the reality of nothingness—of *le néant*—a nothingness of life she claims to live in. In her apparent madness she wants to dance while accompanied by laughter and tears, for life, as she would have it, is both nothingness and being, and the two should dance together.

Of course, Juana la Loca and Cisneros are closer to understanding than one might have supposed: the one is the mirror-image of the other. The Queen, despite her arguments and her insistent tone of rebuttal, is able to express with precision what Cisneros cannot utter, whether out of fear or out of moral cowardice. They are both concerned with the meaning of life and death, of power, of renunciation, and of indifference. Moreover, Juana la Loca is a symbol of spiritual suicide, toward which Cisneros is moving. She is more clearly defined in the play than Cisneros, although after her appearance we understand finally the Queen's reflection in the Cardinal, and we finally understand him. There is, however, a basic difference between the two characters. Juana la Loca has ceased to exist as a normal human because, with the death of her husband, she has lost the meaning of sensual passion, and she longs for death. Cisneros, on the other hand, longs for spiritual passion after death, but he is torn between the ecstasy of God and the ecstasy of life. When death finally does come to Cisneros, it is a death imposed by Montherlant as a dramatic convenience and not a death resulting from treason.

In *Le Cardinal d'Espagne* Montherlant again makes effective use of silent dramatic action, as he does in *La Reine morte* and *Port-Royal;* again, such silent action is made more forceful by his use of symbolism. The sharply contrasting clothing of Cisneros—his robes cover a hair shirt and he wears sandals—remind us of his continual yearning for a godly ideal through sacrifice and renunciation, on the one hand, and of his absorbing involvement with the temporal world, the "mud" in Montherlantian vocabulary. Juana la Loca constantly drinks from an earthenware bowl meant to symbolize her love for her husband King Philippe. Her dress, which suggests that of a cloistered nun, underlines the sense of her temporal renunciation, of her spiritual suicide. At yet another level Montherlant delineates character more effectively without dialogue than with it. Juana la Loca's madness—or is it really the stark reality of her sanity?—is most clearly revealed in the strange "protocole" scene preceding the private interview with Cisneros.[13] When Juana la Loca kills a fly with her fichu in the middle of their serious conversation, we may or may not be convinced of her sanity. At the play's end Montherlant suggests the coming destruction of Cisneros by off-stage barking of dogs, and later by the barking of a single dog. To this background he adds the sound of horses and the Angelus.

In addition to the dramatic effects wrought by symbolism and by silent dramatic action, Montherlant adds yet another dimension, the contrast of colors. We have already seen how the Archbishop and his entourage in *Port-Royal,* all brilliantly garbed, form a startling contrast with the sisters of Port-Royal and especially with the sisters from other Orders entirely dressed in black. In *Le Cardinal d'Espagne* Juana la Loca's somber dress is in balance with Cisneros' red robes. Indeed, the Cardinal's robes appear in constant relief against a background of sobriety and somberness. The sudden flashes of brilliant color which repeatedly appear, as they do in *Port-Royal,* underline the human and earthly qualities that Montherlant wishes us to see in Cisneros.

I have written that *Le Cardinal d'Espagne* is an extension of *La Reine morte.* As drama it is also superior to it. First, the characters of *Le Cardinal d'Espagne* are drawn with an extreme attention to clarity; they explain the sense of Montherlant's hero and his dilemma because transitions are stated in the dramatic framework. Second, Montherlant has developed his language to such an extent that candor replaces enigma, and we can know Cisneros and Juana la Loca as separate entities and as reflections of each other: his language, always rich, is maintained at a high level, it is unvarying and it is noble. Finally, his use of symbolism, whether by means of object, motion, or gesture—all in silent action—enhances the meaning of this drama far more effectively than it does, for example, in *La Reine morte.* In *Le Cardinal d'Espagne* Montherlant demonstrates that he has mastered dramatic technique and that he is comfortable with it. By contrast, *La Reine morte* or even *Le Maître de Santiago* appear as first essays of the technique rather than as final masterworks.

VIII La Guerre civile

The important influence of pagan Rome on Montherlant, or more accurately, the mystique of Rome that Montherlant has lived with since the age of nine, explains the creation of *La Guerre civile.* What is surprising is the knowledge that he has never published a true "Roman play" or "Roman novel"—that is, works with Rome itself as subject or background. This supposed lack may be explained by underlining again, if briefly, the direction of the mystique. While Rome is at the heart of the mystique, it is a romanticized view of what Rome may have been rather than a realistic view of a historical Rome. Of course, Montherlant's mystique developed at a time when he was not academically attuned to history; at the present time Montherlant possesses a thorough knowledge of Roman culture, although it may well not conform to his original, and more sensitive, feeling for it. It is the expansion and extension of the mystique that explains his novelistic and dramatic themes, for Montherlant is concerned with the whole Mediterranean world where pagan Rome ruled, and with Roman vestiges in the cultures of Renaissance Spain and Italy.

Even *La Guerre civile* (1965), often referred to as his "Roman play," is Roman only in the sense that all of the themes stem from the mystique. The play, as Montherlant explains in his "Postface" to *La Guerre civile,* is a third attempt to explore the subject of civil war.[14] It is beside the point to insist on his use of Roman history, for he might well have used a contemporary moment to achieve his goal. His first attempt, still in manuscript form, was a novel, "Le Préfet Spendius," written around 1957, intended to treat the struggle between pagan and Christian Rome. He indicates that his novel *Le Chaos et la nuit* is the second work devoted to the subject of civil war; he considers it, then, the first published work touching on the theme. One may wish to argue with Montherlant over the matter, for *Le Chaos et la nuit,* while it does depict the aftermath of Spain's Revolution, is not precisely about civil war itself: it studies Celestino's inner strife, and Spain serves only as a backdrop.

In *La Guerre civile* Montherlant takes up Roman history as it unfolds in the camps of Caesar and Pompey near Dyrrachium in 48 B.C., just before the decisive battle of Pharsalus. The play bears the stamp of Montherlantian character types. Laetorius, General of Caesar's army, already displaying a penchant for treason in the first act, joins the army of Pompey in the final two acts. He is balanced by Cato, Pompey's General, who is an officer far more secure in his political convictions and far more sensitive to Pompey's intrigues. Caesar and Pompey also balance each other, although indirectly, since Caesar never appears on stage. It is made clear, however, that both military-political leaders have an equal dose of ambition, pride, and especially love of power. But

Montherlant draws attention from the humanity of these men and directs our view rather to the noble purpose of civil war.

In this work I find that the mature Montherlant has come full circle to rejoin the romantic and youthful *L'Exil, Fils de personne,* and *Demain il fera jour;* the work is directly related to *Le Songe.* The play breathes an ecstasy of war, an ecstasy made entirely familiar in the first portions of *Le Songe.* It studies men—there are no women in *La Guerre civile*—whose vision of life is constantly determined and limited by the immediacy of death. Death is far more meaningful than life, or so the play states. Montherlant implies that civil war is a sacrificial arena that strengthens the racial structure of a national society. More important than the voices of the visible players is the voice of Civil War, an unseen personification having a woman's voice—and the Chorus, also unseen, with a male voice. Both voices are in balance and give the play an amplitude not offered by the dialogue. The voice of Civil War soars over the play and gives to it the definition of its unique morality: generosity is a portion of treason; for example, the Greeks became slaves when they ceased to kill each other; amnesty nullifies the sense of civil war. Civil War declares from offstage that it will create a victory and then destroy the victory.[15] The Chorus, on the other hand, seems at first to speak with the voice of reason. Later, it seems the voice of pragmatism, and finally that of history as it forecasts the coming events at Pharsalus.

One is tempted to listen only to the voices of Civil War and the Chorus, voices which underline the sense of the play. Of all of the human, and visible, characters in *La Guerre civile,* Cato of Pompey's camp portrays most clearly the soldier who is *engagé,* most closely involved with Pompey's purposes. His involvement, however, is an intelligent one, for he is capable of rationalizing the vast possibilities imposed by either victory or defeat. He also possesses the ability to visualize clearly his own destruction in the event of defeat, as well as his moral destruction in the event of victory. Endowed with a character resembling that of Malatesta, hence inspired but unstable, he longs, for example, for a retreat in Athens because there he may find human wisdom and truth victorious over human madness and folly. Cato's words suggest that *La Guerre civile* is essentially a moralistic work proving the moral inefficacy of civil war. But the voices of the treacherous Laetorius, of the ambitious Pompey, expose a truth altogether contrary to

"Christian" morality. War, especially civil war, is for these Romans the natural instrument to achieve grandeur, just as international war, as we have seen in Montherlant's earlier works, is a natural path toward the realization of the self. It would be unnatural, within such a framework, to deny man his wars and prevent his killing of fellow men.

Hence, *La Guerre civile* is remarkably devoid of "Christian" morality and will offend those who oppose wars for any reason. For Montherlant, however, war is a phenomenon with which man must live, as common, as natural as procreation itself. Few can deny Montherlant's essential honesty in depicting civil war as a fact of life. Rather than concluding that *La Guerre civile* is too negative, too narrow and overly emphatic, I prefer to see the play as a honest attempt to examine an important theme with frankness; the brutality that pervades the drama is the familiar brutality of war. If nihilism also pervades the play, it is properly a part of dramatic horror. Man as he is interests Montherlant, and such a man is always a more fascinating study than man as he is supposed to be. Certainly, Montherlant's main contribution to the stage is his portrait of reality, often brutal. If his plays often make us feel anxious about the human condition, we have only to recall that Montherlant insists that anxious people are right in being so.

As for the structure of *La Guerre civile,* it is disappointing to find a somewhat erratic plot development. There are too many asides and certainly the characters of this play speak at too great length. A two-act structure might better have served the purposes of the drama, and a disciplined reduction of dialogue might have focused attention more directly upon the play's sense. But an evening with Montherlant at the theater always requires patience: the reward obliterates memory of structural weaknesses.

CHAPTER 6

Montherlant Critic of His Own Work

I *The Creative Artist and His Public*

TWO major obstacles confront the creative artist, no matter what his chosen medium of expression may be. First, he must begin, maintain, and somehow terminate his work in accordance with his own intimate concepts of art. In doing so he may have to dominate, as did Mallarmé, the inevitably dismal blank page; if he is a painter he may have to master the bleakness of untouched canvas; or if he is a sculptor, for example, he may have to force form on massive lumps of clay. All art, without exception, has its solemn measure of infinite possibility, although such infinity is always rigorously limited physically: the edge of the canvas, the borders of the page, the laws of music, together with the whole gamut of disciplines ordered by taste, reason, and appropriateness. Once the work is begun, it can be overpowering to such an extent that it possesses the artist rather than the other way around; the artist may think that he is in command of his creative form when in reality he is being led by it. There are dangers inherent in creativity: the superfluous word, the overstatement in watercolor, the insidious additional dab of clay. A masterpiece is judged first as a whole: the infinite is reduced to a comprehensible finite form, first by the artist and then by his judges. But the judges of creativity have only the final form—as well as its concepts—to look at. What they miss, and what we all may miss, is the process of creativity known only to the artist. This is a singular loss in a very real sense, of course, but it is not an obstacle to the understanding, appreciation, or sharing of the created work.

The artist must stand figuratively in the shadows of his creation and hope that his public will rationally or intuitively seize upon the same vision that he imagines he controls. The masterpiece is forced to speak for itself. Yet here we are faced with the problem of supreme misunderstanding and even of indifference in an artist-public relationship: only the naïve and untried artist hopes for a sensitivity of comprehension on the part of the public that equals his own. This second obstacle confronting the artist—misunderstanding in interpretation—appears as entirely obvious until we realize that even a common understanding—that is, a parallel vision of value seen both by artist and his public—may be largely a gesture of renunciation of an esthetic stand, or perhaps a gratuitous bow to respectability. If the artist depicts deep sorrow in his work, he may well have spelled out the sense of that sorrow for his public, which is, after all, capable of knowing the gamut of that emotion. But what he cannot do, despite all of his efforts, is interpret the precise tone, tenor, and scope of his sorrow; he cannot define the depths of its wellsprings or the myriad manifestations that led to or from it. The artist's sorrow is personal: an accurate communication with its nature and with the artist must remain forever the artist's private affair. We all know, of course, how the artistic tools of communication hamper understanding. The musical note, held to the restrictive laws of music, can go only so far as a symbol of expression. Words are particularly restrictive, as poets have always realized. Symbolism, for example, arose from the very real wish to make language unrestrictive, free, and capable of communicating the infinite sensations of the mind. But symbolism,.surrealism, as well as the many other isms of artists, are gestures toward communication; the problem remains unresolved.

II *Toward an Understanding: Montherlant's Explications*

There is one way out. The artist can create what he determines to be a finished masterpiece and then supplement his work with multiple explanations, notes, memorabilia, documentations, and so on, all of which he intends as a larger clarification of the original masterpiece. It is an "in other words" procedure meant usually to help rather than hinder understanding. Such is Montherlant's technique. But it is one that for a long time has dismayed readers and critics and often alienated those who have found values in his works. What is especially disconcerting is Montherlant's apparent need to defend his entire literary corpus as if it needed a major defense. Of course, young artists, impatient to be understood and appreciated, rail against an unfavorable press and express privately what the critics should have understood. But the mature Montherlant, always at odds with the literary élite of Paris and even with critics abroad, is unable to relax even for a moment: he cannot permit each work to speak for itself. Critical interpretation of his works must necessarily be a reflection of his own interpretation. He acknowledges favorable criticism that may match to some degree his own, and he favors imaginative views that go beyond his own first thoughts—provided, of course, that his original vision is never altered. Such imaginative interpretation, always risky at best, must possess a grandeur of concept equal to the author's; it may perhaps augment his own interpretation, especially if it opens new channels of thought at higher levels. Montherlant's notes and commentaries are usually published with the works themselves; some have been published separately and later gathered in the Pléiade editions; and the *Carnets* also contain his opinions of his own works. He is unreserved in his vehemence and vitriol directed against those who see something different in his works, especially against critics who indulge in the hypothetical or often find his many notes unrewarding.

Typical of his method of annotation is his inclusion, together with the play *La Reine morte,* of a preliminary bibliography and "discographie"; there is also a brief letter to Vaudoyer of the Comédie Française explaining the nature of his inspiration. What follows the play's text, however, is anything but brief: "Comment fut écrite *La Reine morte,*" Roger Jeanne's "Quand nos prisonniers jouaient *La Reine morte,*" "Allocution prononcée par Henry de Montherlant à l'occasion de la centième de *La Reine morte,*" "La Création de *La Reine morte,*" and finally, "En relisant *La Reine morte.*" [1] The letter to Vaudoyer is dated 1942, and the articles and essays following the play range in date from 1943 to 1954. It goes without saying that readers should acknowledge with appreciation all notes and bibliographical references leading to a clear understanding of the author's purpose. But Montherlant does not stop there: most of the twenty-two pages of annotations in the Pléiade edition contain a restatement of the play itself—as if no one had really understood its dramatic sense. This restatement is a curious procedure since Montherlant is conscious of the umbilical cord between creator and work that must finally be severed. In severing it, however, Montherlant dotes exclusively on favorable criticism and favorable public reaction.

He is most appreciative of Roger Jeanne's reporting of the primitive production of *La Reine morte* by prisoners of war. He is delighted by Madeleine Renaud's first interpretation of Inés de Castro.[2] By contrast, Montherlant may have overextended himself in his enthusiastic reporting of Renée Faure's portrayal of the

Infanta: she plunges onto the stage, he writes, like a small black bull from Navarre entering the arena. Her creation of a masculinized Infanta—a depiction readily understood by the public—is further described at length. Montherlant means her to be far different from the Infantas of Spain on view at the Prado. When Renée Faure cries out the Infanta's irritation and indignation, she reminds Montherlant of a mare he has seen in Tunisia, a mare whose mouth is forced back by the bit and from which flows a foam that attracts birds. This depiction of the Infanta obviously attracts Montherlant's attention more than Madeleine Renaud's interpretation of Inés, and his emphasis seems out of proportion with reality. Perhaps, in retrospect, the Infanta does interest him more even than Ferrante.

In his "En relisant *La Reine morte*" Montherlant further compounds his crime of obfuscation. He admits on the one hand that a literary work is diminished by the author's commentaries, but on the other hand he expresses what he terms the double humility of having produced a work that might have been more beautiful; he feels diminished in relation to his own work.[3] I am not sure that his latter view is altogether in harmony with the sense of humility. I sense, rather, his surprise, at least in 1954, on realizing the multiplicity of possible interpretations his play *La Reine morte* is capable of inspiring. He suggests in his essay that the inspirational "breath" of women—as a dramatic force—is contained in *La Reine morte.*[4] Yet women scarcely dominate in the play. Is Montherlant trying to be misleading, or is he simply misled, or are we perhaps misled? Admitting that the Infanta is the rarest of the play's characters, he accurately states that Ferrante is the dominating force of the drama; but he gives the Infanta and Ferrante an equal value, and their equal value is not visible within the play. Montherlant, however, mentions the important influence of "women," in the plural. We must then conclude that he does not overlook Inés de Castro. But Inés is a static character, almost faceless, and certainly less than inspirational; in deforming the legend of Inés de Castro, Montherlant reduces her to a symbol in the play's last scene. Elsewhere, she plays no real part in psychological motivation; she is essential only when she listens to Ferrante's soliloquy-like outpourings and thereby becomes unwittingly the enemy of a man who destroys those who know too much about him.

The reasons for Ferrante's destruction of Inés de Castro are also revealed by Montherlant in his commentaries, probably to counteract opinion that finds Ferrante's action gratuitous—an *acte gratuit*—rather than motivated. But Montherlant's explanations may not necessarily correspond to those of his audience. He insists that Ferrante kills Inés because he is at the mercy of his own weakness. His act, then, stems from lack of logic. The playwright also indicates that Ferrante kills because he is by nature sadistic and because he has a hatred of life.[5] But Montherlant has not developed, within the framework of the three acts, the character of Ferrante to such a high degree that the audience can understand the sense of his motivation. In claiming an author's privilege of auto-interpretation, Montherlant can deform his own work, shifting rôles and meanings to make them match his own logic. What he does do in the more than twenty pages of commentary is create the framework of a second *Reine morte*. One wonders if the skeletal new version, stemming from the articles and notes, might not have been superior to the version seen at the Comédie Française.

I have already noted his tendency to explain characters—the Infanta as a raging bull, for example—by way of poetic imagery. He explains the whole of *La Reine morte*, insofar as its construction is concerned, by a similar technique: it is a flower with a stem. The stem, indicating the rigid direction of dramatic action, ends as a flower in the third act, which, by comparison, makes the first two acts seem barren.[6] Such use of poetic interpretation to explain his play tends to undermine critical clarity.

A further irritant in his critical method is his footnote. At the conclusion of "En relisant *La Reine morte*" Montherlant refers with certain justification to the symbolic treason of Dino del Moro. In a footnote he explains that children betray the adults in *La Reine morte* and *Fils de personne*, but that adults betray the children in *La Ville dont le prince est un enfant*.[7] Indeed, treason is a major theme in his work, yet I recall that Gillou (of *Fils de personne*) is rather a victim of Georges Carrion; Montherlant's notes point out that Gillou is at the mercy of parental sacrifice. Besides, Gillou is entirely too lacking in character to understand the full implications of treason or of sacrifice. Similarly, Soubrier and Sevrais, the two boys of *La Ville*, are not precisely the victims of adult treason: they are victims of a systematic morality that cannot embrace the different and the unusual. If the masters of the Catholic school are traitors, they are traitors to God. However, I think that Montherlant is always writing of unwitting treason rather than of planned, premeditated treason. Certainly the two concepts of the term are not always clear in the author's notes. But the note I have cited may serve to underline the waywardness of some of Montherlant's views that emerge now and again to deflect the focus of understanding.

As yet another form of auto-interpretation, Montherlant cites the findings of critics either to forward or elaborate his own views, or else to undermine their opinions for the amusement of his readers. His painstaking documentation of *La Ville dont le prince est un enfant* seems an extraordinary plea for understanding of the moral issues in the play, but his plea is made in a century when any facet of human conduct is considered worthy of esthetic treatment.[8] Here Montherlant emerges, despite the obviously primitive tone of his work, as more puritan than the Puritans, hence more "American," if we are to believe the frequently voiced opinion that only Americans are incapable of studying human aberrations and that a national psychology prevents Americans from understanding the nature of the human animal. In his defense of *La Ville* he quotes at length from his own published articles concerning the play, cites the foreign press and the foreign reactions, always as a defense. Far more strange is his highly elaborate statement exposing his hesitation at seeing the play performed at the Comédie Française. He quotes in full a letter addressed to Monseigneur Feltin seeking the latter's opinion—which turned out to be unfavorable. In setting forth the entire controversy—if that word correctly describes the one-sided war of the conscience—Montherlant in effect establishes indirectly what he considers to be the value of the play. In view of Montherlant's departure from religious faith, although not from Catholic symbolism, his explications appear as vaguely insincere protestations about a matter that no longer has any importance. His Catholicism, not of dogma and discipline, is as muted today as his concern for caste, for Paris, and for civilization's erosions. He does arrive, however, at a critical method through such protestations, for the suspense stimulated by the "Postface" is manifest: it should be examined by those wishing to know yet another dimension of Montherlant. Although extra-contextual, the suspense has a dramatic ring about it; it summons up memories of a Tartuffe or a Trissotin who appear in Molière's comedies only after arousing the audience's intense curiosity.

Montherlant also attacks all interpreters of his works, whether they be professional writers or professional critics, or even both. The outpouring of venom has existed throughout his entire career; it is most often encountered in his *Carnets,* but in various notes and maxims as well. The force of his attack, of course, largely depends on the force of critical disapproval. In the case of two plays—*La Reine morte* and *Port-Royal,* to name but two works highly acclaimed generally by both audiences and critics—his related commentaries and notes are benign, mature, and settled. But *Don Juan* may serve as one example of a clear departure from his unusual benign nature. To be sure, he perhaps made an error in using the play as a vehicle to counter criticism. After the first performance of *Don Juan,* devastatingly adverse critical opinion ricocheted back and forth across the Parisian literary world, and it became a sort of *cause célèbre* abroad as well as in France. Montherlant's reply to the critical world, contained as usual in his notes, begins with his own interpretation of the legend and with his own sense of the dramatic meaning.[9] Seen as a bizarre and perhaps fascinating version of the legend, his *Don Juan* might have served as an example of ingenious theatrical technique (or even as an artist's joke, if only to punctuate a long line of Don Juans of unequal merit). But Montherlant is essentially humorless and insists on a serious interpretation that must ultimately appall the viewer or reader. Humorless in his attitude toward his *Don Juan,* he underlines the play's bad taste. In emphasizing, for example, Don Juan's main trait as one of mobility—a mobility of character and a corresponding vivacity of speech—he creates a character not realized in the play itself. And he claims further that the public must possess a mobility necessary to an understanding of the Don Juan character he has created. Montherlant is undoubtedly using a new term to describe the multifaceted man that pervades his work, but he fails to realize that his Don Juan is almost without character. Moreover, he suggests that Don Juan is *méridional,* having the Spanish characteristics of the Sevillano; elsewhere, he indicates that his hero is another manifestation of the Renaissance Malatesta; and he concludes that his Don Juan reflects, except for the quality of the *pathétique,* the Italian character. Indeed, he discusses the first act as written in the Italian manner.[10]

To answer comments on his interpretation he states that the play is at once bitter and farcical.[11] Again, in a paragraph strongly suggestive of out-dated nineteenth century criticism, he claims that his work is essentially tragic. What Montherlant has done, as he has for many of his plays, is create through his notes a second play: here he creates a second *Don Juan* that bears little resemblance to the legend and little resemblance to his original play as the audience understands it. But his notes are interesting: they come often as a vast surprise even to those who care only about the superficial manipulation of plot. He forgets, nonetheless, that the play itself must reveal its psychological truths by means of its own devices, devices made self-evident through artistic techniques within the scope of the performance.

Toward the end of his notes on *Don Juan* Montherlant departs from his explications and begins to berate the critics who constantly misinterpret his works.[12] He refers to them as *clercs,* as clerks in a derogatory sense; he thinks of them as being better able to decipher numbers than to undertake the delicate task of deciphering art forms. In part, of course, he is reacting to those critics who have accused him of being Don Juan. Admittedly, Montherlant has often been the victim of unjustified comments and attacks, especially whenever criticism insists too much on the hypothesis, usually stated as fact, that his entire literary work is a variable collection of personal anecdotes clothed in the garb of Rome, Spain, and Renaissance Italy.

To a large degree Montherlant has created his own monster. Caesar, Seville, Malatesta, and Papal Rome, the young bulls in the cult of the corrida, as well as all of the ancient Mediterranean myths, appear constantly in his works, his notes, his references, and his essays. There lies his first love and all of the symbolism of an ideal that must be an important part of his own life. Of course, against the symbolized ideal, Janus-like, is the phenomenon of what must be his personal spleen. He is so engrossed with the idealism he has created that his extra-literary world seems psychologically ill by contrast. His France is without the dignity, or the *dignitas,* of an idealized, non-existent Rome. Paris, immersed in an apparent search for material values, is too remote from him. France of *Le Songe,* if France is really an issue of major importance, is beyond his understanding. Spain of *Les Bestiaires* is a treasonous land in *Le Chaos et la nuit.* Montherlant is an ultra-conservative who rejects the modern as valueless; but he is also a sensitive idealist whose worlds are *songes,* entirely unreal. It is no wonder that Montherlant finds himself constantly at odds with those who are impatient with such nebulous idealism.

It is on a different level that Montherlant reveals his truest talent: he is the master of psychological portrayal. Critics, however, have often been impatient with his syncretic, amoral man who can be Roman, Spaniard, or Renaissance Italian, or even a Frenchman. In all his portrayals the hero (or the non-hero) emerges as much the same sort of person; his heroes, at least, tend to be larger than life, often to the point of being unable to communicate. Critics, in relating his characterizations to Montherlant's own person, have greatly erred, I feel, especially when they treat works written after the lyric period. It is not surprising that Montherlant rebels at being called Don Juan, Malatesta, Celestino, and so on. Touches of Montherlant's personality may indeed appear here and there in his work, but his heroes are not mirror-images of the writer. Like all writers he makes use of experience, his own or experience gained in observation, as a foundation for his creativity. How could one possibly explain the whole of *Port-Royal,* a Léon de Coantré or a Celestino, if Montherlant portrayed himself? He is as evasive in his character portrayals as he is in his auto-criticism, for he defies close description and is supremely proud of his ability to slip from one rôle into another. The critic who attempts to pinpoint the personal life of the author in his works risks Montherlant's wrath, of course; and the author manages to muddy the sense of his art by never permitting it to be viewed outside of his shadow. His game invites ambivalence.

I have mentioned Montherlant's evasiveness. In terms of auto-criticism, however, his evasiveness may simply be forgetfulness. In 1953, for example, he states that *Port-Royal* completes a Catholic trilogy which includes *Le Maître de Santiago* and *La Ville dont le prince est un enfant;* his sense of trilogy is based on three subjects the works treat: the knightly order, the school, and the convent.[13] Yet in a "Postface" to *Le Maître de Santiago,* dated 1946, he writes that the play is an *auto sacramental,* and in the same category he places two other works. One, *Don Fadrique,* was abandoned in 1929; the other is *Port-Royal.* Whether through forgetfulness or shifting viewpoint, Montherlant may leave us with several conflicting definitions of his work. It is quite possible that he finds both definitions to be true today, especially since his interpretation of "Catholic" and of *auto sacramental* suggests that the terms are synonymous with "religious."

III *The Burden of Critical Responsibility*

I have presented only a few examples of the problems created by Montherlant as critic of his own work. His method is somewhat insidious because unwary readers may be persuaded by the intensity of his arguments—as well as by the potent imagery of his better poetic passages—to accept only his conclusions. He does have the critic's ability to penetrate, to ferret out esthetic values, and he has the poet's keen imagination to seize on possibility. But he often fails to see his own work as it appears to others; his argumentations and embellishments often form new realms of realities quite apart from his works. Hence, the reader of Montherlant, or the audience, must assume the burden of responsibility. He must seek his own values and truths without Montherlant's help. I do not wish to conclude that Montherlant's notes and commentaries and certain of his essays are without value, of course, but it should be understood that they are not always within his original focus.

On the other hand, there is an entirely favorable side to Montherlant as critic of his own work. He does strive diligently to furnish his readers with extensive documentation, especially with reference to his historical plays. His notes on *Le Maître de Santiago,* and more especially those on *Port-Royal, Le Cardinal d'Espagne,* and *La Guerre civile,* are entirely necessary for understanding the plays in historical context; his notes also clarify his departures from historicity. As a critic, Montherlant is always conscious of the need to recapture the atmosphere of the past, as he does magnificently in *Port-Royal* and in *Le Cardinal d'Espagne.*

CHAPTER 7

Conclusion

HENRY DE MONTHERLANT has chosen a solitary road to follow in the world of letters and in society; he shuns commerce with his contemporaries, refuses to dignify his social milieu, shuts himself off from a wide communication with his public, and abhors the fatal concept of "playing the game." He has depended so heavily on a mystique of the past that he fails to understand that his worlds—the pagan-mythical Mediterranean and the latter-day civilizations of Rome, Renaissance Italy, and Spain—are fictions of his acutely developed imagination. His worlds are Montherlantian states of mind, and they are so fragilely conceived by him that they crumble when exposed to truth, especially to his sense of the truth. But from out of these states of mind emerges the universal man who appears in each of his works as hero or non-hero, together with mirror-images, the vast pullulations of the master prototype. Hence, while he fails to develop a philosophy worthy of the name, he nevertheless creates a unified psychological study of man's condition as Montherlant understands it.

We are not always comfortable with his definitions, of course. But they are not comfortable for Montherlant, either. His universal man is far better able to cope with the dilemma of life when he is young and remote from the dilemma's resolution in death. Sensuously devoted to the animalistic, sentimentally attached to cults and visible symbols, and divorced from warm human contact, his universal man is irrevocably doomed with the passing of time: he must turn away from the sensual become meaningless, he must know the mindlessness of superficial symbolism, and he must inevitably find himself enveloped in a desperate nihilism of isolation. Nothing prepares him for the end of life. Each character, from Alban de Bricoule to Cisneros, is foredoomed to a symbolic or real self-destruction; in this sense, suicide is perhaps the major theme of Montherlant's works. Certainly, Montherlant is one of the great masters of pessimism of the twentieth century: it is a pessimism without solution, moreover, because in devising his universal man—a man of total possibility—Montherlant fails to give him the sense of his own humanity in a sea of humanity. He is incomplete because he has no human contact with his fellow man. In creating Costals, for example, Montherlant builds an enormous case history that is often alien to the human.

Yet Montherlant's study of man, even if it does occasionally stray from our vision of reality, is bound to endure as one of the best of the twentieth century. His works will last because they are poetic statements of the human condition as envisioned in no fixed point of time. I am certain that his better plays will serve as the primary conveyer of his concepts because of their disciplined form and their richness of language. To a lesser degree, his novels and poetry support his drama, at least thematically, but they are less original. Montherlant has not mastered the structure of the novel, nor has he created a new structure. His plays alone, however, are sufficient to maintain his high reputation in the world of letters.

It is well known that Montherlant keeps completed and partly completed manuscripts in his desk drawers. We may look forward to new works and reworkings of earlier publications, as well as to explications of both. We may also expect his usual acerbity addressed to his critics, whether they are right or wrong. I earnestly hope that his forthcoming publications will have the scope, the grandeur, and the poetry of *Le Cardinal d'Espagne*.

Notes and References

PREFACE

1. A bibliography of limited editions (to 1959) is contained in Henri Perruchot, *Montherlant* (Paris: Gallimard, 1959), pp. 288–292.

2. See Bibliography.

CHAPTER ONE

1. See "Index biographique" in Henry de Montherlant, *Théâtre* ("Bibliothèque de la Pléiade" [Paris: Gallimard, 1958]), entry for 1955, p. xli. (This edition hereafter noted as *Théâtre,* Pléiade.)

2. J.-N. Faure-Biguet, *Montherlant, homme de la Renaissance* (Paris: Plon, 1925), and Jean Datain, *Montherlant et l'héritage de la Renaissance* (Paris: Amiot-Dumont, 1956).

3. See Henry de Montherlant, "Saint-Simon" (*Textes sous une occupation*) in *Essais,* Bibliothèque de la Pléiade (Paris: Gallimard, 1963), pp. 1503–1515. (This edition hereafter noted as *Essais,* Pléiade.)

4. According to Sartre, writers are all more or less Jansenists. See Jean-Paul Sartre, "Qu'est-ce que la littérature?" in *Situations, II* (Paris: Gallimard, 1948), p. 251: "Nous sommes donc jansénistes parce que l'époque nous a faits tels et, comme elle nous a fait toucher nos limites, je dirai que nous sommes tous des écrivains métaphysiciens."

5. See Michel Mohrt, *Montherlant "homme libre"* (Paris: Gallimard, 1943) and Michel de Saint Pierre, *Montherlant bourreau de soi-même* (Paris: Gallimard, 1949).

6. Montherlant, "Syncrétisme et alternance" (*Aux fontaines du désir*) in *Essais,* Pléiade, pp. 235–245.

7. Cf. Montherlant's "Avant-propos" to *Service inutile* in *Essais,* Pléiade, pp. 571–592.

8. Montherlant, "Syncrétisme et alternance," p. 238.

9. *Ibid.,* p. 238: "Goethe et Attila émanent d'une seule source d'énergie universelle. Phénomènes de la nature, comme tels ils sont solidaires l'un de l'autre." (All translations are my own.)

10. *Ibid.,* p. 238: "Combattons Attila, mais en connaissant son utilité supérieure, combattons-le avec une complaisance profonde, et, pour tout dire, combattons-le en l'aimant."

11. *Ibid.,* p. 239; "Je persiste à croire qu'être humain, c'est comprendre tous les mouvements des hommes."

12. Unless we accept Sartre's view (note 4, above).

13. Montherlant, "Syncrétisme et alternance," p. 420: "Etre à la fois, ou plutôt faire alterner en soi, la Bête et l'Ange, la vie corporelle et charnelle et la vie intellectuelle et morale, que l'homme le veuille ou non, la nature l'y forcera, qui est toute alternances, qui est toute contradictions et détentes."

14. *Ibid.*, p. 242: "Nous voyons que *tout est vrai*."

15. *Ibid.*, p. 241: "La violence, les superstitions, l'arbitraire, tous les instincts, toutes les ivresses, tout le troupeau parfumé des passions, que ma raison et ma conscience morale rejettent, rentrent dans la place, à la dérobée, rappelés par ma poésie."

16. *Ibid.*, p. 241: "Je suis poète, je ne suis même que cela, et j'ai besoin d'aimer et de vivre toute la diversité du monde et tous ses prétendus contraires, parce qu'ils sont la matière de ma poésie, qui mourrait d'inanition dans un univers où ne régneraient que le vrai et le juste, comme nous mourrions de soif si nous ne buvions que de l'eau chimiquement pure."

17. The term *dominio*, from the Spanish, is applied by Montherlant to all living creatures, including the self, as well as to all of life's situations; it implies both a taming and a possession.

18. See Montherlant, *Le Cardinal d'Espagne* (Paris: Gallimard, 1960), pp. 230–232 (Note IV): "Les Deux Pourpres."

19. Faure-Biguet indicates Montherlant's interest in bullfighting at the age of nine.

20. Simone de Beauvoir, *Le Deuxième Sexe* (Paris: Gallimard, 1949). Simone de Beauvoir insists that the Montherlantian hero is never face to face with an equal or even with entirely authentic human beings.

CHAPTER TWO

1. Henri Perruchot also uses the term "historiette."

2. Drama of the lyric period is treated elsewhere in this book.

3. Cf. Pierre Sipriot, *Montherlant par lui-même* (Paris: Editions du Seuil, 1963), pp. 178–179. In "Sur ma mère" Montherlant describes his mother and especially his relationship with her.

4. I feel it necessary to separate the lyric works (novels and other fiction) from the later novels, which Montherlant calls his "romans-romans," or his objective novels.

5. Montherlant, *Le Songe* in *Romans et oeuvres de fiction non théâtrales* ("Bibliothèque de la Pléiade" [Paris: Gallimard, 1959]), p. 9: "—Mon cerveau s'est épuisé tandis que mon corps refleurissait! Je m'arrête de penser! Je rejette la couronne d'épines! Il est nécessaire que je me repose dans l'action." (This edition hereafter noted as *Romans*, Pléiade.)

6. *Ibid.*, p. 8: "Pourquoi cette défiance de moi-même? Je ne compte que sur moi et ne consulte que moi."

7. *Ibid.*, p. 11: Douce is "inutile en dehors de l'amour."

8. *Ibid.*, p. 163: Chapter XIV is titled "Tout vient des êtres."

9. *Ibid.*, p. 174: "Ah! depuis longtemps il savait que c'étaient des êtres . . . qui fondaient sa conscience morale, et que toujours il en arrive à une question de personnes."

10. *Ibid.*, p. 174: "Il n'y avait plus la raison de l'acte, ni la récompense de l'acte. Mais, dur et nu, avec à son terme la mort, et par-devant Alban qui regardait cela un petit brin, puis frissonait, faisait 'non' de la tête. Pardonné soit-il."

11. *Ibid.*, p. 181: "Comme un chat qui refuse de s'approcher de la chatte, sa mère, qui agonise; comme un fauve se précipite sur le dompteur qui est tombé; comme toute la basse-cour vient donner un coup de bec à la poule parce qu'elle saigne, à mesure qu'il [Alban] la voyait touchée, il lui en voulait davantage. Elle retira sa main, qu'elle avait portée devant ses yeux, et soudain, la voyant si laide dans les pleurs, il la désira."

12. *Ibid.*, p. 205: "Et quand nous nous serons quittés, du bout des doigts, excédés l'un de l'autre et nous détestant tout bas, je n'aurai pas fini encore de la trahir. L'instant qu'elle était nue et mienne se brouillera dans ma mémoire comme un songe, car je vieillis et n'imprime plus bien mes bonheurs. Chaque corps que je croiserai, combien médiocre auprès du sien, me donnera le coup de lance d'amour. Rien ne me semblera désirable que ce qui n'est pas ma Dominique. Je renierai ce que j'ai eu en songeant à ce que je ne puis avoir. . . . Ah! triste amour! Un bock de bière en été donne davantage de bonheur."

13. Montherlant, *Les Olympiques* in *Romans*, Pléiade, pp. 307–308: ". . . l'ordre du sport ne demande pas la suppression de toute sensibilité, de toute délicatesse, de tout abandon, de toute compassion. Il demande qu'ils passent au second rang, et puissent être en cas de besoin jugulés."

14. There are remarkable parallels between this work and *Le Chaos et la nuit:* flight to Spain and disenchantment followed by flight to France.

15. Montherlant, *Les Bestiaires* in *Romans*, Pléiade, p. 520: "La masse de l'église . . . dominait, toute proche et de toute sa hauteur, comme si la plaza et elle étaient d'un seul tenant. Ainsi aux arènes de Nîmes un clocher, aux arènes d'Arles une statue de la Vierge pointent au-dessus de l'enceinte. Et Alban, qui aime la paix spirituelle, se sentait plein d'une joie douce à ce nouveau témoignage de Mithra et Christ reconciliés."

16. *Ibid.*, p. 520: "Les bestiaires, accoudés, ne disaient rien. Dans le silence, la sonnette d'un cabestro tinta, comme pour l'Elévation."

17. *Ibid.*, p. 565: "La divinité du sang fumait comme de la chaleur."

18. *Ibid.*, p. 579: "Fau de sang e la mort pèr coungreia la vido./ Lou Creatour meme a soufert."

19. *Ibid.*, p. 566: "Et il [Alban] entre dans l'église, et il remercie Dieu d'avoir permis qu'il ait vécu cette journée grande auprès de quelqu'un [Jesús] pour qui il a tant de sympathie."

20. Montherlant, *La Petite Infante de Castille* in *Romans*, Pléiade. The legend is related on p. 604 and expanded on pp. 619–620.

21. *Ibid.*, p. 600: "Est-ce une conséquence de mon culte du Soleil? Je n'aime que le teint brun, et ce que je ne peux faire autrement que d'appeler l'*odeur du teint brun*, odeur, chaleur de jeunesse virulente, de jeunesse plus proche de la nature que la nôtre. Odeur de sexualité. Toute cette belle jeunesse est 'affranchie.' "

CHAPTER THREE

1. Jean de Beer, *Montherlant, ou l'homme encombré de Dieu* (Paris: Flammarion, 1963). Cf. also Michel Mohrt's work on Montherlant.

2. See especially Lucille Becker, "Pessimism and Nihilism in the Plays of Henry de Montherlant," *Yale French Studies*, XXIX (1962), 88–91.

3. Montherlant, *Les Célibataires* in *Romans*, Pléiade, p. 756: "Après deux ans elle [l'affaire] était en faillite. Levier avait été honnête tant que Léon avait été sérieux. Du jour où Léon, incapable d'application ou seulement d'esprit de suite, d'ailleurs obsédé par la femme, cessa de venir, tourna résolument à l'amateur titré. . . ."

4. *Ibid.*, p. 758: "Léon de Coantré, pendant ces trois ans, avait vécu chez sa mère. De travailler il ne fut pas question. Mme de Coantré pensait qu'il se couperait la gorge au premier mot qu'elle dirait là-dessus. Evidemment, le jour où il s'était coupé la gorge, ou avait fait semblant, il avait eu une fameuse idée. Ce nouvel état, de vivre sous l'aile de sa mère, défrayé de tout, et dans une insouciance de petit garçon, fut de son goût. Il ne demanda qu'à le conserver. Il le conserva vingt ans."

5. *Ibid.*, p. 761: "Recueilli dès la vingtième année par sa soeur, selon le voeu de leur père, Elie cessa de s'occuper de quoi que ce fût au monde, qui n'était pas ses paperasses. Il éblouissait la famille par l'étendue de ses connaissances. La famille était bien incapable de faire le départ entre l'instruction et l'intelligence, et de se rendre compte qu'Elie était un imbécile doué d'une bonne mémoire."

6. In Montherlant's works insanity frequently speaks logical truth. Cf. Juana la Loca (Jeanne la Folle) in *Le Cardinal d'Espagne*.

7. *Les Célibataires*, p. 813: "Les 'sauvages' de la trentième année sont les amers de la cinquantaine."

8. *Ibid.*, p. 815: ". . . ce qu'il y a de tragique chez les anxieux, c'est qu'ils ont toujours raison de l'être."

9. *Ibid.*, p. 827: "Mais le grand goût de M. de Coantré était toujours de dormir. Toujours il avait aimé s'étendre sur son lit dans la journée. Tantôt, il prenait alors en main un crayon et un papier, et était censé provoquer et noter des idées touchant l'amélioration de sa situation matérielle: il appelait cela *tirer des plans.* Tantôt, il y restait à l'état végétatif. . . ."

10. *Ibid.*, p. 902: "Il avait compris la *recette* qui lui permettait d'échapper à sa détresse: cette recette était la fierté." Or again: "Et toutes ses misères, automatiquement, passaient du plan du sordide à celui de la hauteur, où elles cessaient de lui faire mal."

11. The last sentence is typical of Montherlant's poetic prose: "Chaque fois que M. Octave et sa soeur sont à Fréville, la tombe de Léon de Coantré est fleurie de fleurs toujours fraîches" (p. 914).

12. For example: "Et nous allons dire ce qu'il [Elie] était devenu" (p. 761). The "nous" is the novelist.

13. Montherlant, *Les Jeunes Filles* in *Romans,* Pléiade, p. 943: "Il s'agit d'un composé d'affection et de désir, qui n'est pas l'amour." Or again: "Et enfin je n'aime pas qu'on ait besoin de moi, intellectuellement, 'sentimentalement,' ou charnellement. L'inexplicable plaisir que des êtres éprouvent de ma présence, les diminue à mes yeux."

14. *Ibid.*, pp. 1009–1010: "C'est par inconscience que la majorité des hommes se marient, comme c'est par inconscience qu'ils font la guerre. On frémit à la pensée de ce que deviendrait la société, si les hommes se mettaient à se gouverner par leur raison: elle périrait . . . sous nos yeux, périr de leur intelligence les peuples trop intelligents."

15. *Ibid.*, pp. 1040–1041: ". . . 1° parce qu'il trouvait convenable que, dans la même minute où il caressait pour la première fois une jeune personne, il en désirait une autre; 2° parce que, donnant l'apparence du sommeil, il était impossible qu'elle ne levât pas en lui la pensée d'abuser de ce sommeil; 3° parce qu'il lui semblait que, pour éprouver une telle extase d'un phénomène aussi insipide que cette musique, il fallait qu'elle fût détraquée; . . ."

16. The same question of *vous* and *tu* arises in *Encore un instant de bonheur* and in *L'Histoire d'amour de "La Rose de sable."*

17. Montherlant, *Pitié pour les femmes* in *Romans,* Pléiade, pp. 1146–1147: "L'inhumanité de Costals ne venait pas de ce qu'il ne pût ressentir des sentiments humains, mais, au contraire, de ce qu'il pût les ressentir tous indifféremment, à volonté, comme s'il ne fallait pour chacun d'eux que presser le bouton approprié."

18. Montherlant, *Les Lépreuses* in *Romans,* Pléiade, p. 1491: "Et en quelle femme se réfugie Costals? Aberration! Il se réfugie en Solange. Il va vers celle qui lui a fait tant de mal, comme le chien que son maître frappe se réfugie en rampant aux pieds de ce maître."

19. *Ibid.*, p. 1523: "On commence à vous connaître. Vous êtes un illusioniste. Vous donnez l'illusion d'être toujours changeant, à mille

faces. Et vous êtes toujours le même, désespérément le même. Vous retombez toujours sur le même accord, comme la musique de Mozart. Vous revenez avec vos mêmes tics d'il y a deux ans. Stupide vous êtes, stupide vous resterez."

CHAPTER FOUR

1. Montherlant, *Théâtre,* Pléiade, pp. 937–954.
2. *Ibid.*, p. 397.
3. *Ibid.*
4. Montherlant, *Celles qu'on prend dans ses bras* in *Théâtre,* Pléiade, p. 802: "M. Ravier aime qui ne l'aime pas, et sans doute n'aime pas qui l'aime, comme vous ne l'aimez pas, qui vous aime, et peut-être aimez quelqu'un qui ne vous aime pas." Mlle Andriot's words explain the sense of "love" in Montherlant's works.
5. Montherlant, *Brocéliande* (Paris: Gallimard, 1956), pp. 7–9. Montherlant explains that "*Brocéliande* est une pièce triste dans une enveloppe de demi-gaîeté."
6. *Ibid.*, p. 148: "La comédie doit finir gaiement, car il faut avouer que notre histoire est une véritable comédie: du lever jusqu'au baisser du rideau, on a nagé dans le burlesque" (III.ii).
7. In III.iii.
8. *Brocéliande,* p. 58: Madame: "Et, dites-moi, comment descendez-vous de Saint Louis?" Persilès: "Par les femmes. Evidemment, il aurait mieux valu que . . ." (I.iii).
9. *Ibid.*, p. 150: "Don Quichotte, quand il a cessé d'être fou . . ." (III.iii).

CHAPTER FIVE

1. Montherlant's notes on his theater are in *Théâtre,* Pléiade.
2. J. D. M. Ford, [Camões'] *Os Lusíadas* (Cambridge: Harvard University Press, 1946); the legend of Inés de Castro is found in Canto III, cxviii–cxliii.
3. Luis Vélez de Guevara, *Reinar después de morir* in *BAE* (Madrid: Rivadeyra, 1881), XLV, 109–123.
4. See Robert B. Johnson, "The Ferrante Image in Montherlant's *La Reine morte,*" *The French Review,* XXXVI (January, 1963), 255–259.
5. See Montherlant, "En relisant *La Reine morte*" in *Théâtre,* Pléiade, pp. 253–259.
6. Begun in 1943, produced in 1950. Date indicated is that of first publication.
7. Note Montherlant's concept of charity in *Théâtre,* Pléiade, pp. 671–672, Note III.
8. See *Théâtre,* Pléiade, p. 659; and "Le Maître de Santiago est-il chrétien?", pp. 674–675.

9. Montherlant, Preface to *Port-Royal* in *Théâtre,* Pléiade, pp. 959–967.

10. Cf. Jean de Beer, *Montherlant, ou l'homme encombré de Dieu* (Paris: Flammarion, 1963), pp. 405–412.

11. Montherlant, *Don Juan* (Paris: Gallimard, 1958), p. 181.

12. Montherlant, *Le Cardinal d'Espagne* (Paris: Gallimard, 1960), pp. 211–215.

13. *Le Cardinal d'Espagne,* II.iii.

14. Montherlant, *La Guerre civile* (Paris: Gallimard, 1965), pp. 185–194.

15. This is the same theme expressed in *Port-Royal.*

CHAPTER SIX

1. Montherlant, *Théâtre,* Pléiade, pp. 131–134, 237–259.
2. *Ibid.,* p. 250.
3. *Ibid.,* p. 253.
4. *Ibid.*
5. *Ibid.,* pp. 256–257.
6. *Ibid.,* p. 258.
7. *Ibid.,* note 1.
8. *Ibid.,* pp. 937–954.
9. Montherlant, *Don Juan* (Paris: Gallimard, 1958), pp. 175–184.
10. *Ibid.,* p. 179.
11. *Ibid.,* p. 181.
12. *Ibid.,* p. 182.
13. Montherlant, *Théâtre,* Pléiade, p. 959.

Selected Bibliography

Abbreviated references for primary sources contained in Pléiade editions:

Théâtre, Pléiade: *Théâtre* ("Bibliothèque de la Pléiade"). Paris: Gallimard, 1958.

Romans, Pléiade: *Romans et oeuvres de fiction non théâtrales* ("Bibliothèque de la Pléiade"). Paris: Gallimard, 1959.

Essais, Pléiade: *Essais* ("Bibliothèque de la Pléiade"). Paris: Gallimard, 1963.

PRIMARY SOURCES

(Not indicated are limited editions too numerous to list; for complete bibliography to 1959 see Henri Perruchot, *Montherlant* [Paris: Gallimard, 1959].)

La Relève du matin. Essays. Paris: Société littéraire de France, 1920. In *Essais,* Pléiade. Portions in *Selected Essays.* Trans. JOHN WEIGHTMAN. New York: Macmillan, 1960; London: Weidenfeld and Nicolson, 1960.

Le Songe. Novel. Paris: Grasset, 1922. In *Romans,* Pléiade. Trans. as *The Dream* by TERENCE KILMARTIN. New York: Macmillan, 1963.

Les Olympiques. "Historiettes," with some dramatic and poetic form. *Première Olympique: Le Paradis à l'ombre des épées.* Paris: Grasset, 1924. *Deuxième Olympique: Les Onze devant la porte dorée.* Paris: Grasset, 1924. In *Romans,* Pléiade. Portions in *Selected Essays.* Trans. JOHN WEIGHTMAN. New York: Macmillan, 1960; London: Weidenfeld and Nicolson, 1960.

Chant funèbre pour les morts de Verdun. Essay. Paris: Grasset, 1924. In *Essais,* Pléiade.

Les Bestiaires. Novel. Paris: Mornay, 1926. In *Romans,* Pléiade. Trans. as *The Matador* by PETER WILES. London: Elek Books, 1957.

Aux fontaines du désir. Essays. Paris: Grasset, 1927. In *Essais,* Pléiade.

La Petite Infante de Castille. "Historiette." Paris: Grasset, 1929. In *Romans,* Pléiade.

L'Exil. Play. Paris: Editions du Capitole, 1929. In *Théâtre,* Pléiade.

Mors et vita. Essays. Paris: Grasset, 1932. In *Essais,* Pléiade. Portions in

Selected Essays. Trans. JOHN WEIGHTMAN. New York: Macmillan, 1960; London: Weidenfeld and Nicolson, 1960.

Encore un instant de bonheur. Poems. Paris: Grasset, 1934. In *Romans*, Pléiade.

Les Célibataires. Novel. Paris: Grasset, 1934. In *Romans*, Pléiade. Trans. as *The Bachelors* by TERENCE KILMARTIN. New York: Macmillan, 1961; London: Weidenfeld and Nicolson, 1960. Also trans. as *Perish in Their Pride* by THOMAS MCGREEVY. New York: Knopf, 1936; and as *Lament for the Death of an Upper Class*. London: J. Miles, 1935.

Service inutile. Essays. Paris: Grasset, 1935. In *Essais*, Pléiade. Portions in *Selected Essays*. Trans. JOHN WEIGHTMAN. New York: Macmillan, 1960; London: Weidenfeld and Nicolson, 1960.

Pasiphaé. Dramatic poem. Tunis: Editions des Cahiers de Barbarie, 1936. In *Théâtre*, Pléiade.

Les Jeunes Filles. Tetralogy of novels. In *Romans*, Pléiade.

Les Jeunes Filles. Paris: Grasset, 1936. Trans. as *Young Girls* in *Pity for Women*. Trans. THOMAS MCGREEVY. New York: Knopf, 1938; London: Routledge, 1937.

Pitié pour les femmes. Paris: Grasset, 1936. *Pity for Women*. Trans. JOHN RODKER. New York: Knopf, 1938; London: Routledge, 1937.

Le Démon du bien. Paris: Grasset, 1937. Trans. as *Demon of Good* in *Costals and the Hippogriff*. Trans. JOHN RODKER. New York: Knopf, 1940; London: Routledge, 1940.

Les Lépreuses. Paris: Grasset, 1939. Trans. as *The Lepers* in *Costals and the Hippogriff*. Trans. JOHN RODKER. New York: Knopf, 1940; London: Routledge, 1940.

L'Equinoxe de septembre. Essays. Paris: Grasset, 1938. In *Essais*, Pléiade. Portions in *Selected Essays*. Trans. JOHN WEIGHTMAN. New York: Macmillan, 1960; London: Weidenfeld and Nicolson, 1960.

Le Solstice de juin. Essays. Paris: Grasset, 1941. In *Essais*, Pléiade.

La Reine morte. Play. Paris: Henri Lefebvre, 1942. In *Théâtre*, Pléiade. Trans. as *Queen after Death* in *The Master of Santiago and Four Other Plays*. Trans. JONATHAN GRIFFIN. New York: Knopf, 1951; London: Routledge, 1951.

Fils de personne. Play. Paris: Gallimard, 1944. In *Théâtre*, Pléiade. Trans. as *No Man's Son* in *The Master of Santiago and Four Other Plays*. Trans. JONATHAN GRIFFIN. New York: Knopf, 1951; London: Routledge, 1951.

Un Incompris. Play. Paris: Gallimard, 1944. In *Théâtre*, Pléiade.

Un Voyageur solitaire est un diable. Essays. Paris: Henri Lefebvre, 1945. In *Essais*, Pléiade.

Malatesta. Play. Lausanne: Marguerat, 1946. In *Théâtre*, Pléiade.

Trans. as *Malatesta* in *The Master of Santiago and Four Other Plays.* Trans. JONATHAN GRIFFIN. New York: Knopf, 1951; London: Routledge, 1951.

Le Maître de Santiago. Play. Paris: Gallimard, 1947. In *Théâtre,* Pléiade. Trans. as *The Master of Santiago (and Four Other Plays)* by JONATHAN GRIFFIN. New York: Knopf, 1951; London: Routledge, 1951.

Demain il fera jour. Play. Paris: Gallimard, 1949. In *Théâtre,* Pléiade. Trans. as *Tomorrow the Dawn* in *The Master of Santiago and Four Other Plays.* Trans. JONATHAN GRIFFIN. New York: Knopf, 1951; London: Routledge, 1951.

Celles qu'on prend dans ses bras. Play. Paris: Editions Dominique Wapler, 1950. In *Théâtre,* Pléiade.

La Ville dont le prince est un enfant. Play. Paris: Gallimard, 1951. In *Théâtre,* Pléiade.

Textes sous une occupation. Essays. Paris: Gallimard, 1953. In *Essais,* Pléiade. Portions in *Selected Essays.* Trans. JOHN WEIGHTMAN. New York: Macmillan, 1960; London: Weidenfeld and Nicolson, 1960.

L'Histoire d'amour de "La Rose de sable." Novelette drawn from the unpublished *La Rose de sable.* Paris: Editions des Deux-Rives, 1954. Trans. as *Desert Love* by ALEC BROWN. New York: Noonday Press, 1958; London: Elek Books, 1957.

Port-Royal. Play. Paris: Henri Lefebvre, 1954. In *Théâtre,* Pléiade.

Brocéliande. Play. Paris: Gallimard, 1956.

Carnets 1930–1944. Notebooks. In *Essais,* Pléiade.

Carnets XXIX–XXXV (19 février 1935–11 janvier 1939). Paris: La Table Ronde, 1947.

Carnets XLII–XLIII (1er janvier 1942–31 décembre 1943). Paris: La Table Ronde, 1948.

Carnets XXII–XXVIII (23 avril 1932–22 novembre 1934). Paris: La Table Ronde, 1955.

Carnets XIX–XXI (19 septembre 1930–26 avril 1932). Paris: La Table Ronde, 1956.

Don Juan. Play. Paris: Gallimard, 1958.

Le Cardinal d'Espagne. Play. Paris: Gallimard, 1960.

Le Chaos et la nuit. Novel. Paris: Gallimard, 1963. Trans. as *Chaos and Night* by TERENCE KILMARTIN. New York: Macmillan, 1964.

Discours de réception à l'Académie Française. Reception address at the French Academy. Paris: Gallimard, 1963. Contains reply of M. le Duc de Lévis Mirepoix.

La Guerre civile. Play. Paris: Gallimard, 1965.

Va jouer avec cette poussière (Carnets 1958–1964). Notebooks. Paris: Gallimard, 1966.

SECONDARY SOURCES

(A list of critical works on Montherlant would be too extensive to set forth in full; the following is a partial list.)

BARO, GENE. "Montherlant and the Morals of Adjustment," *The Sewanee Review,* LXIX (1961), 704–708. A good discussion of Montherlant's inconsistencies.

BEAUVOIR, SIMONE DE. *Le Deuxième Sexe.* Paris: Gallimard, 1949. Trans. as *The Second Sex* by H. H. PARSHLEY. New York: Knopf, 1953. Indispensable for the study of Montherlant's women; contains good arguments but false conclusions partly based upon prejudices.

BECKER, LUCILLE. "Pessimism and Nihilism in the Plays of Henry de Montherlant," *Yale French Studies,* XXIX (1962), 88–91. A brief but excellent treatment that should be examined by students of Montherlant's theater.

BEER, JEAN DE. *Montherlant, ou l'homme encombré de Dieu.* Paris: Flammarion, 1963. With commentary in notes and brief conclusion by Montherlant. As Montherlant correctly states it, this work is too concerned with hypotheses; but he does little to clarify issues posed by De Beer.

BOISDEFFRE, PIERRE DE. *Métamorphose de la littérature.* Paris: Editions Alsatia, 1951. Of particular interest is "Henry de Montherlant ou le chevalier du néant," pp. 229–279. It contains a novel view of *Les Célibataires.*

CHASSANG, ARSÈNE. "Montherlant critique de son oeuvre," *La Table Ronde,* No. 155 (November, 1960), 172–182. Generally favors Montherlant's critical judgment of his own work, but with several exceptions.

CLOUARD, HENRI. "Montherlant moraliste," *La Table Ronde,* No. 155 (November, 1960), 208–213. A brief examination of *la morale* in Montherlant's works.

CRUICKSHANK, JOHN. *Montherlant.* London: Oliver and Boyd, 1964. A good general introduction to the study of the life and work of Montherlant; excellent chapter on art and style (Chapter VI).

DATAIN, JEAN. *Montherlant et l'héritage de la Renaissance* (*suivi de Le Sang des Malatesta*). Paris: Amiot-Dumont, 1956. Contains also Louis de Saint-Pierre's *Montherlant et les généalogistes.* A good and entirely favorable study of Montherlant's *Malatesta.*

DEBRIE-PANEL, NICOLE. *Montherlant, l'art et l'amour.* Lyon: E. Vitte, 1960. An enthusiastic defense of Montherlant's treatment of women and the theme of love. Less scholarly than Sandelion's work (see below).

DOMINIQUE, PIERRE. *Quatre Hommes entre vingt* (Montherlant, Morand, Cocteau, Drieu La Rochelle). Paris: Le Divan, 1924.

An early view of Montherlant's "Romanization," with some false conclusions.

FAURE-BIGUET, J.-F. *Montherlant homme de la Renaissance.* Paris: Plon, 1925. Long before publication of *Malatesta,* Montherlant's boyhood friend traces in detail Renaissance traits in the man and in the author.

———. *Les Enfances de Montherlant.* Paris: Henri Lefebvre, 1948. Also includes *Montherlant homme de la Renaissance.* Faure-Biguet's association with Montherlant permits him to trace the years 1905–1916.

GUICHARNAUD, JACQUES. *Modern French Theater from Giraudoux to Beckett.* New Haven: Yale University Press, 1961. Of special interest is Chapter 4: "The Agony of Solitary Souls: Henry de Montherlant," pp. 93–111. An excellent, although brief view of Montherlant's theater as understood by an actor, playwright, and scholar.

HELL, HENRI. "Montherlant et l'Afrique du Nord," *La Table Ronde,* No. 155 (November, 1960), 71–74. An excellent point of departure for students interested in the lyric period.

JACCARD, PIERRE. *Trois Contemporains: Mauriac, Chardonne, Montherlant.* Lausanne: Editions La Concorde, 1945. An interesting view of Montherlant's actions and attitudes during the years of World War II.

JOHNSON, ROBERT B. "Definitions of Youth in the Theater of Montherlant," *Modern Language Journal,* XLVII (April, 1963), 149–154. A summary of Montherlant's concepts of quality and mediocrity in youth.

———. "The Ferrante Image in Montherlant's *La Reine morte,*" *The French Review,* XXXVI (January, 1963), 255–259. A study of mirror-images in the play.

KASTERSKA, MARYA. *Pages catholiques.* Paris: Plon, 1947. A collection of quotations from Montherlant's work designed to show his Catholicism. Of main interest is the brief introductory text.

LAPRADE, JACQUES DE. *Le Théâtre de Montherlant.* Paris: La Jeune Parque, 1950. Treats *La Reine morte, Le Maître de Santiago, Malatesta, Fils de personne, Demain il fera jour,* and *L'Exil.* The book poses many problems of criticism but too often offers no solutions. Comments on Catholicism are good.

———. Preface to *Théâtre* in "Bibliothèque de la Pléiade." Paris: Gallimard, 1958. An entirely favorable view of the theater.

MATZNEFF, GABRIEL. "Pessimisme et nihilisme chez Montherlant," *La Table Ronde,* No. 155 (November, 1960), 214–222. More specifically treats the subject as related to *Le Cardinal d'Espagne.*

MOHRT, MICHEL. *Montherlant "homme libre."* Paris: Gallimard, 1943. Especially good treatment in "Le Héros" and "L'Homme libre."

MORREALE, GERALD. "'Alternance' and Montherlant's Aesthetics." *The French Review,* XXXVII (May, 1964), 626–636. An excellent study of the sense of alternation.

NORRISH, P. J. "Montherlant's Conception of the Tragic Hero," *French Studies,* XIV (1960), 18–37. A study of the static quality in Montherlant's heroes; interesting comparison with heroes of Corneille and Racine.

PERRUCHOT, HENRI. *Montherlant.* Paris: Gallimard, 1959. A general work and entirely favorable. Of particular use to students because of an extensive bibliography through 1959, including listing of limited editions.

———. *La Haine des masques.* Paris: La Table Ronde, 1955. A good introductory work for an understanding of Montherlant, particularly with regard to his concept of the universal man.

SAINT-PIERRE, LOUIS DE. *Montherlant et les généalogistes.* See Jean Datain. *Montherlant et l'héritage de la Renaissance.* Paris: Amiot-Dumont, 1956. A study of Montherlant's genealogy.

SAINT-PIERRE, MICHEL DE. *Montherlant bourreau de soi-même.* Paris: Gallimard, 1949. A good treatment of Montherlant's theater of desolation, especially of *Fils de personne* and *Demain il fera jour.* Brief, but perceptive.

SAINT-ROBERT, PHILIPPE DE. "Montherlant et le catholicisme," *La Table Ronde,* No. 155 (November, 1960), 38–47. A generous look at Montherlant's faith.

SANDELION, JEANNE. *Montherlant et les femmes.* Paris: Plon, 1950. This is perhaps the best study to date on the subject of women in Montherlant's work; it should be read in conjunction with Simone de Beauvoir's *Le Deuxième Sexe* (see above).

SECRÉTAIN, ROGER. Preface to *Romans et oeuvres de fiction non théâtrales* in "Bibliothèque de la Pléiade." Paris: Gallimard, 1959. A general and generous view of Montherlant.

SIMON, PIERRE-HENRI. *Procès du héros.* Paris: Editions du Seuil, 1950. A negative report on the Montherlantian hero.

SIPRIOT, PIERRE. *Montherlant par lui-même.* Paris: Editions du Seuil, 1963. Excellent for students beginning their study of Montherlant; contains illustrative passages from the works and photographs.

———. Preface to *Essais* in "Bibliothèque de la Pléiade." Paris: Gallimard, 1963. Sipriot traces what he claims to be the main themes in Montherlant's works.

ZERAFFA, MICHEL. "'Les Célibataires' ou les ruses du réalisme," *La Table Ronde,* No. 155 (November, 1960), 118–120. An interesting, often curious, interpretation of Montherlant's first major novel.

Index